STUDY GUIDE

RECLAIM
Your
Soul

DESTINY IMAGE BOOKS BY DR. CINDY TRIMM

Reclaim Your Soul

40 Days to Reclaiming Your Soul

Reclaim Your Soul Curriculum

The 40 Day Soul Fast

40 Days to Discovering the Real You

40 Day Soul Fast Curriculum

DR. CINDY TRIMM

STUDY GUIDE

RECLAIM
Your
Soul

DESTINY IMAGE® PUBLISHERS, INC.

P.O. Box 310, Shippensburg, PA 17257-0310

"Promoting Inspired Lives."

This book and all other Destiny Image, Revival Press, MercyPlace, Fresh Bread, Destiny Image Fiction, and Treasure House books are available at Christian bookstores and distributors worldwide.

For a U.S. bookstore nearest you, call 1-800-722-6774.

For more information on foreign distributors, call 717-532-3040.

Reach us on the Internet: www.destinyimage.com.

ISBN 13 TP: 978-0-7684-4251-9

For Worldwide Distribution, Printed in the U.S.A.

1 2 3 4 5 6 7 8 / 18 17 16 15 14

CONTENTS

INTRODUCTION FOR PARTICIPANTS

Welcome to the *best days of your life*—ones filled with the joy of living free from anything hampering the life of your soul. Your destiny changes the moment you start to change your decision-making strategies. This is the "soul" purpose of the *Reclaim Your Soul* book and study guide. These resources are designed to equip you with strategies to break old cycles—those destructive patterns created by habit-forming soul attachments—and thereby empower you to experience a whole new lifestyle of resiliency.

Too many believers visit the altar more than they sustain a lifestyle of freedom. This has been the case for years in the body of Christ. We try to live off of yesterday's "altar call experience" and are disappointed when it fades. Maybe someone agreed with you in prayer for deliverance, "breakthrough," or inner healing. Perhaps you attended an event or conference, and someone prayed for you to experience freedom, joy, peace, or victory. There is a chance that it lasted for a season, but more than likely it didn't last until the next day.

What is the usual strategy? Find another person to agree with us in prayer? Visit another conference? Pursue another experience?

God uses experiences to initiate a process. Experiences were never designed to be a process unto themselves. An experience should lead to something. While those special moments of coming forward and laying things down before the Lord at the altar are quite necessary, a day must come when the experience becomes a *lifestyle*.

People can pray for you, but they can't tell you who you are. This is an exchange that takes place between you and God alone—and this is the journey I want to take you on in the *Reclaim Your Soul* study. It's all about being empowered to change—when *you* decide to change—*whenever* you desire to change.

Change is gradual, and best understood in a simple parable posed as a question: "How do you eat an elephant?" Answer: "One bite at a time." This is how we will attack the subject of reclaiming your soul. Over the next 40 days, you will have the opportunity to identify the things that are restricting your progress, growth, and development.

To continue with the analogy, I want to touch on what we know about domesticated elephants. The elephant is the world's most powerful animal. Zookeepers and elephant trainers typically strap a thin metal chain to a grown elephant's leg, and then attach the other end to a small wooden peg that's hammered into the ground to restrict their movement. Although the ten-foot-tall, ten-thousand-pound elephant—which can uproot a tree as easily as a human being can break a toothpick—could easily snap the flimsy chain and uproot the wooden peg, escaping to freedom with minimal effort, it doesn't. In fact, the elephant never even tries. Why? Because when the elephant was a baby, its trainers used the exact same type of thin chain, strapped it around its leg, and fastened the other end of the chain to a wooden peg in the ground. At that time, the chain and peg were strong enough to restrain the baby elephant. When it tried to break away, the metal chain would restrict its movement. Within a short period, the baby elephant was conditioned not to try to escape because escaping was not possible.

Later, when the elephant matures, it perceives that the thin chain and small peg make it impossible to escape. Of course, this is not true—but it is what this powerhouse of an animal *believes* to be true. It doesn't matter that the once small baby is now ten thousand pounds; it is the elephant's self-limiting belief about the power of the attachment that prevails.

If you think about it, we are all like elephants. We are all incredibly powerful individuals attached to our own kind of mental, spiritual, social, and cultural chains—soul ties and attachments that hold us back. But you can break free and live with a new freedom in Christ Jesus.

Over the eight weeks ahead, I want to arm you with new strategies for a new season of true freedom in Christ and a lifetime of resilience. The old season is the one where you went to the altar, had the pastor pray, felt a rush, maybe experienced seasonal freedom, but then the cycle of bondage continued—sometimes worse. Enough with that! The new season is all about breaking cycles, building new boundaries, and experiencing the life of resiliency that God always meant for you to enjoy (see John 10:10).

Championing your journey toward empowerment,

—Dr. Cindy Trimm

HOW TO USE THIS STUDY GUIDE

WEEKLY GROUP SESSIONS

You can either join a group or pull together a group of your friends, sisters and brothers in the Lord, or colleagues. These individuals will make up your inner-circle support group that will provide invaluable insights and accountability as you work through the weekly activities (see Eccles. 4:9-10; Ps. 133:1-3).

Ideally, you will attend weekly sessions with your group or class. During this time you will watch one of the eight DVD sessions, discuss what you learned, pray together, and participate in helpful empowerment exercises. In order to get the most out of your experience, you *must* be willing to go beyond information and open yourself up to transformation.

This happens through *participation*. Although participatory exercises are not always comfortable, the ones in this study have been crafted with your health and growth in mind. As we have learned throughout our experiences with *The 40 Day Soul Fast* group curriculum, it is in the stretching—and sometimes squirming—that true growth and lasting freedom is achieved.

And, although the journey is intensely personal, it is in the sharing, the observing, the acknowledging, the trusting, and the humble and transparent releasing with others who are all struggling, searching, believing, and hoping just like you. Reclaiming your soul is most effectively and joyously done in community.

SESSION STRUCTURE

Below is the set structure for each session in the *Reclaim Your Soul* study.

Summary

This is a short summary briefly introducing participants to that session's topic.

Learn

Watch Dr. Trimm's *Video Session*.

Discuss

Go through a series of *Group Discussion Questions*. These are structured intentionally, but are not all mandatory. If there is a certain question that seems to be directing the group/class sessions and the Holy Spirit is moving powerfully in that context, yield to His movement and stay on that particular subject.

Empower

After the *Group Discussion Questions*, allocate 10 to 15 minutes to do the empowerment exercise. This gives individuals and groups the opportunity to interact with what they have just learned.

Sustain

These are the *Daily Reflection Exercises*. Depending on how much time you have available to commit, they can take from 5 minutes to 25 minutes.

Daily Exercises

The daily reflection exercises are inspiring devotions meant to reinforce, not repackage, what you learned in the video sessions. The material is new and was written with one goal in mind—to help you *sustain* transformation every day of your life.

The time required for each day's exercises will vary, although the reading and simple meditation segment shouldn't take more than five to ten minutes on any given day.

One Step toward Resiliency

Once again, to get the maximum impact from your *Reclaim Your Soul* experience, it is recommended that you spend 10 to 15 minutes focusing specifically on the *One Step toward Resiliency* at the end of each daily reflection.

After the prompt, you will find ample writing space. This is designed to turn your "study guide" into a valuable personal resource. I envision this becoming a journal that, upon completion, does not end up resting on a shelf somewhere, but is a vital handbook to your transformation process.

The greatest jewels of revelation that fill this book will not be what is written in typed print, but the insights and reflections that you record during your journey.

RECLAIM YOUR SOUL: BOOK AND JOURNAL

This study is meant as a supplement to the *Reclaim Your Soul* book. To truly benefit from the study, you should read the book prior to doing the study (while working through the companion journal). This eight-week study is built on the principles presented in the book and journal. However, if this is not possible, the DVD study will still be meaningful and greatly beneficial if done in the context of a small group.

If this is the case for you, you might endeavor to read the book in conjunction with the study or shortly after completing the study. You will *not* get regurgitated, repackaged content. Yes, some of the key concepts will be repeated. That is intentional for the purpose of reinforcement. However, each of the *Reclaim Your Soul* elements provides fresh revelation on how to break cycles and behavioral patterns keeping you from living more resiliently.

Session One

YOU START THE TRANSFORMATION

*"You must be the change you wish to
see in the world." —*GANDHI

*The moment you invite change is the
moment you embrace your destiny.*

SUMMARY

In order to reclaim your soul, or understand what this process even means, you need to first recognize that true change begins with God. With God, life shouldn't just happen to you; you should happen to life. This study is all about taking back the personal power you exchanged through entertaining a soul tie.

Rather than blaming the person or thing that you are attached to, assuming it is their responsibility to do something about your destiny, you need to step up—or at least "wake up" as Christ admonished when He said, *"Awake, you who sleep…see that you walk circumspectly…do not be unwise, but understand what the will of the Lord is"* (Eph. 5:14-17). The moment you take responsibility for where you are in life (or *why* you are where you are) is when you position yourself to move toward where you *want* to be.

Purpose is God's job; destiny is yours. God has a predestined and pre-ordained purpose tailor-made just for you. However, you need to make daily decisions and choices that are in agreement with this purpose in order to position yourself (yes, you must position yourself) to walk out your destiny.

To step into this purpose and give God complete control over your life, you need to *get your soul back* from whomever or whatever you have given it to. This is the journey we are embarking on for the next 40 days/8 weeks. Don't misunderstand—God is the One we must give our souls to. The problem is we can say this, pray it, and sing it, but if we have given our soul away (to anything other than God), we need to get it back so we can, by choice, freely hand it to the only One deserving of our complete surrender.

LEARN

Watch Session 1 of the *Reclaim Your Soul* video series.

Discuss

Engage your group in conversation using the following questions.

1. Read Matthew 16:26. Why do you think God asks us questions? (In this case, Jesus is asking a question.)

2. Read 1 Corinthians 13:11. Why do your strategies for life need to change as you grow and develop?

3. What happens when you try to use immature, old strategies in a new season? Have you ever experienced this in your life?

4. How is taking responsibility for your actions and situations important when it comes to breaking soul ties/attachments? (Instead of always blaming someone else, or some type of external force?)

5. How does your decision to change actually change the people who are in your life?

6. How do you "resemble" those you assemble with? (How do your relationships push you toward or lead you away from your destiny?)

7. In what ways can unhealthy relationships keep you blind to the negative cycles you are currently stuck in?

8. What does the following statement mean to you? *Purpose is determined by God; destiny is determined by you.*

9. How do your daily choices impact your destiny?

EMPOWER

What one thing can you start to change today that will change everything in your life?

So many people neglect the simple power of starting with *one thing*. They mistakenly assume, "Surely, it can't be that easy." While the journey is not always "easy," too many of us never actually step out and embrace the transformation process because they never begin with that "one thing."

Think about it. Reflect. Pray. And *write it down*. One thing. Not ten. Not five. Not fifty. *Change begins with one step.*

SUSTAIN

This week, for about five minutes each day, you will be going through the parable of the prodigal son from Luke 15. We encourage you to read the entire text for yourself. However, for the purpose of these brief exercises, you will be focusing on specific verses for daily reflection and meditation.

Day One

THE SUBSTANCE OF YOUR SOUL

And he said, A certain man had two sons: and
the younger of them said to his father, Father, give
me the portion of goods that falleth to me. And he
divided unto them his living. And not many days
after the younger son gathered all together, and took
his journey into a far country, and there wasted his
substance with riotous living. —Luke 15:11-13, KJV

More than losing money or possessions, the greatest loss that this son experienced was the loss of his soul. This is your true *substance.* Your soul is God's gift to you, constantly affirming who you truly are.

Be aware that the exchanges you make in life—through relationships, commitments, vows, words, etc.—involve your substance, *your soul.* They are not idle or unattached to you. The prodigal son surely thought he was leaving his father's house and was going to try things out on his own. He not only squandered all he had materially and financially, in the process he lost himself. This is what leads to the chain of events we will review in the following days.

As you continue to read the parable of the prodigal son, ask the Holy Spirit for a fresh perspective. In one respect, it is a story about risk and rebellion. In another it is about immaturity and ignorance. At the same time, it is a very profound example of what happens when we lose our soul. Our identity. Our sense of purpose and destiny. Everything falls when we trade our soul for the second-rate, counterfeit pleasures this world boasts of but cannot deliver on.

ONE STEP TOWARD RESILIENCY

Because your soul is your very substance, guard it as the most prized and precious possession. Recognize that it cannot be exchanged for anything, as there is no price tag that can begin to value your worth.

> *The soul is God's gift, offering you constant affirmation of who you truly are.*

_____

_____

_____

_____

_____

_____

_____

_____

_____

_____

_____

Day Two

IN WANT

*And when he had spent all, there arose a
mighty famine in that land; and he began
to be in want.* —LUKE 15:14, KJV

By being "in want," the prodigal son was confronting the loss
that took place. By giving up his soul—his substance—he lost all
bearings on who he was, what he was purposed to do, and where
to go next. He didn't know which way was up or down, and as
a result a series of unhealthy choices and soul ties would follow.
We will explore this later in the week. In the meantime, note the
boy's current posture. He was "in want."

If anything, we need to express some gratitude for this feeling
of being "in want," as it is an internal alarm indicating that our
soul has been compromised. When we are dissatisfied, feeling
empty, and looking around hoping to find *something* to fill the
"void," we need to pause and immediately assess the situation.
Could it be that we are in want because somewhere, at some
point, we gave away our substance? We compromised our soul?

ONE STEP TOWARD RESILIENCY

Get quiet before the Lord and evaluate the state of your soul.

- Do you feel "in want?"

- Are you dissatisfied with where you are in life?

- Do you feel like you are without direction or bearings and are simply "coasting" through life?

Ask the Holy Spirit to reveal where the "want" came from.

> " *Much of what you are looking for...you already have.* "

_____

_____

_____

_____

_____

_____

_____

_____

_____

_____

_____

_____

_____

_____

Day Three

THE QUEST

*Then he went and joined himself to a citizen
of that country; and he sent him into his
fields to feed swine.* —LUKE 15:15

For the next three days, you will reflect on this single verse. It contains a powerful blueprint for what happens when we lose our soul. The "in want" drive is very powerful. If you do not navigate this *soul void* appropriately, it is very easy, if almost inevitable, that you will follow a similar trajectory to the prodigal son's.

Remember, the very thing that can propel you into a wild, destructive chain of events—the feeling of being "in want"—is also your greatest internal alarm. It should cause you to pause, reflect, and evaluate where the loss took place. This internal alarm should have brought the prodigal back home. Sadly, other voices take your feeling of being "in want" as their cue to come and bombard your mind. The enemy will try to make you feel shameful for being "in want." Feelings of hopelessness and unworthiness will compel you to "want" to give up or give over your power—or a fear of rejection may cause you to be "in want" and give in to the demands or negative influences of others. These are lies purposed to keep you spiraling downward. Reject them and move on. Don't be like the prodigal who responded poorly to the invitation of being "in want."

The enemy has one purpose, and that is to keep you trapped in a cycle. The cycle is a snare. It is your prison. It keeps you ineffective. As long as you are prevented from *being you,* you are unable to step into your destiny and offer the world what is uniquely yours to give.

ONE STEP TOWARD RESILIENCY

Start your journey back home, and begin by coming before the Lord and asking Him, *What caused me to be "in want"?*

The Holy Spirit is so faithful to bring these things to our remembrance.

He does *not bring* condemnation or guilt; He only comes with direction, clarity, and wisdom. Any thoughts of shame, condemnation, or fear are from the enemy and must be rejected in Jesus' Name.

Come to the Faithful Shepherd. By stepping into His Presence and reflecting on His affirmations of who you are, you will *not want* (see Ps. 23).

_____

_____

_____

_____

_____

_____

_____

_____

Day Four

SOUL TIES

*Then he went and joined himself to a citizen
of that country; and he sent him into his
fields to feed swine.* —LUKE 15:15

The prodigal son did not respond to the invitation of his internal alarm. He was "in want," but instead of evaluating and recalibrating, he continued to spiral downward. As he did this, he distanced himself further and further from his true identity. This put him in a very dangerous place as he started to look for other things and other people to tell him who he was. This is the birthplace of a dangerous soul tie.

He was "in want" and *went and joined himself to a citizen of that country.* The only One our want should ever compel us to join ourselves to is God. Only He can tell us who we really are, especially if we have surrendered our substance and lost touch with our true self. What the prodigal entered into was a diabolical counterfeit of the exchange that we are called to enjoy with God exclusively. The language in this text is particularly telling of the arrangement that took place. We see that "he went and *joined himself.*"

This soul tie created a codependent, parasitic union, where the prodigal—living in such a state of internal chaos, confusion, and utter purposelessness—was willing to join himself to a complete stranger in order to receive some type of direction or clarity.

ONE STEP TOWARD RESILIENCY

Get quiet before the Lord and reflect on the lifestyle that your "want" has led you into.

- Are you full of purpose and excitement about the future?

- Do you feel like the daily choices you are making are positioning you for the purpose God has for you?

- OR, are there any relationships or attachments in your life that are preventing you from moving toward your dreams and desires?

Be honest with yourself. If you identify any of these types of relationships or attachments, write them down.

> *Everyone you connect to is a mirror of yourself; you will resemble those you assemble with.*

_____

_____

_____

_____

_____

_____

_____

Day Five

BLURRED PURPOSE

*And he sent him into his fields to
feed swine.* —LUKE 15:15

Soul ties become a temporary source of "satisfaction" for the life afflicted with blurred purpose. With no sense of direction, focus, clarity, or purpose, we become desperate for someone or something to tell us what we have been made for. This is an appropriate desire, but again, we see in this story that the desire is being fulfilled in a very unhealthy way. We were created by God *for* God. He is the Author of our purpose, and in turn, He is the One we must run to when our vision becomes blurred or our sense of purpose becomes compromised.

God's door is always open for you. He does not shut it; rather, the enemy does everything he can do to keep us from going through. As mentioned earlier this week, the enemy uses deception and lies to keep us from returning home. Home is the Father's house. This is where we are refreshed by a fresh glimpse of purpose. However, when we become convinced that we cannot go home because the Father will not welcome us, we seek out others to tell us where to go and who we are.

This is the danger of soul ties and, ultimately, the reason we are engaging in this 40-day journey. The prodigal became enmeshed in this union with a *citizen from another country*; he lost all sense of personal worth, identity, and purpose—so much so that he resigned himself to feeding swine. Most likely, the prodigal was a Jewish boy. The thought of him feeding swine—particularly the son of a man of affluence and wealth—was most abhorrent in that culture.

Sadly, when we start allowing people, situations, and even life circumstances to dictate *who we are*, somewhere along the line we will inevitably enter into a soul tie.

As you will learn in the weeks to come, soul ties are not just in regard to relationships. They can be things. Experiences. Memories. Words. Vows. Objects. Instead of becoming paranoid about the soul ties you may or may not have embraced, be encouraged.

ONE STEP TOWARD RESILIENCY

Are you where you want to be today? Carefully consider it.

Do you feel like the life you are living today is the result of intentional choices, or are you where you are because—somewhere along the line—you "joined yourself" with someone in a soul tie?

Maybe it wasn't a person. Maybe it was a business opportunity. Maybe it was a career switch. Maybe it was a relocation. Maybe it was an experience.

These things are not inherently bad; however, anything can become bad or unhealthy for us when we "fall into it" rather than choose it through intention and prayerful consideration.

Is where you *are* where you *want to be* in life? In your marriage? In your relationships? In your finances? In your work?

If not, decide today that you will change—that you will move forward—that you will open your ears to the Holy Spirit's voice over the next 40 days.

Prayer

Lord, You are the Author of my purpose. Show me any soul tie or attachment I have allowed into my life that is keeping me from moving forward and embracing all You have for me.

I surrender to Your instruction. Show me what You need to show me. Tell me what You need to tell me. Your words bring life and healing, and I will listen. Give me strength to obey.

Purpose is determined by God; destiny is determined by you. Your decisions determine your destiny.

HOW MUCH IS YOUR SOUL WORTH?

*For what is a man profited, if he shall gain
the whole world, and lose his own soul?
or what shall a man give in exchange for
his soul?* —MATTHEW 16:26, KJV

Being yourself starts with valuing yourself.

SUMMARY

Jesus does not ask you questions because He needs your answers; He is God. Questions aimed from God to you are for your revelation, understanding, and benefit. The foundational question we will explore during the first half of this study is this: *"For what profit is it to a man if he gains the whole world, and loses his own soul? Or what will a man give in exchange for his soul?"* (Matt. 16:26).

We protect what we value. Likewise, we urgently *reclaim* what we value if it is taken. If someone broke into our home and stole thousands of dollars' worth of fine jewelry, exquisite artwork, technology, etc., we would immediately embark on a mission to reclaim what was stolen. Why? The value. The greater the value, the greater the urgency to reclaim what was taken. Jewelry would take precedence over an old VCR because of the value of the jewelry.

So here is the question: *How much is your soul worth?* In this session, you take a profound and thought-provoking look at Jesus' question in Matthew 16:26. He invites us to consider the priceless value of our souls so that we can live accordingly. This motivates how we protect, nourish, and ultimately reclaim our souls from those who have taken our personal power. The urgency to reclaim our souls intensifies when our understanding of soul value increases.

LEARN

Watch Session 2 of the *Reclaim Your Soul* video series.

DISCUSS

Engage your group in conversation using the following questions.

1.   Why do you think it is important for *you* to value your own soul—more than anyone else does?

2.   Where is one of the key places that change begins?

3.   How is the way that we think linked to how we value our soul/self?

4.   Read Philippians 4:8. According to Paul, what criteria should you use for the thoughts you allow into your mind?

5.   What is the difference between moving ahead and moving on? Can you share an example of an instance in your life when you thought you were moving on, but you were only moving ahead?

6.   What does the following statement mean to you: "Being yourself begins with valuing yourself"?

7.   What are some practical, everyday steps you can take that will help you *value yourself*?

8.   Read Matthew 16:26. What did Dr. Trimm's explanation of the value of the soul (according to the words of Jesus) teach you about *your* value?

EMPOWER

1. Get alone with God, a Bible (in print or on your phone/tablet) and a blank sheet of paper (have paper available). Ask the following questions:

    ▪ What thoughts are you currently thinking about yourself? (How do you see yourself?)

    ▪ Read Philippians 4:8. Write down the characteristics describing the types of thoughts you should be thinking.

    ▪ Now ask yourself, "Am I thinking these kinds of thoughts *about myself*?"

2. What one area can you start thinking differently in this week that will help change the way you value yourself?

SUSTAIN

This week, for about five minutes each day, you will be going through brief exercises. You will be focusing on specific Scripture verses for daily reflection and meditation.

Day Six

VALUE YOUR OWN SOUL

Then he went and joined himself to a citizen
of that country, and he sent him into his
fields to feed swine. —LUKE 15:15

You must value your soul more than anyone else does. Why? Everyone else—no matter who they are or how much they love you—can never value you like you can value yourself. And the way you value yourself ultimately gives others instructions on how you expect them to treat and value you.

The prodigal son communicated loud and clear that he did not value his soul. We witness this in how he quickly joined himself to a "citizen of that country." No deep, mutually beneficial friendship is acknowledged. In fact, Jesus does not even assign the "citizen" a name. If you do not value your own soul, you will have no standard for how you think you should be treated in life.

We see that this citizen did not value the prodigal son's soul or identity because of what he sent him to do—"feed swine." This is not the citizen's fault; it was the son's responsibility. If he had valued his soul, he would not have positioned himself to fall into this state. He would have come to his senses earlier. In truth, he would have never left his father's house. The reality is when he left, he devalued his soul and positioned himself to be exploited, used, and put in a place where he would live beneath his purpose and identity.

There is a place we eventually fall into that redefines our lives because it raises the question of who we are. There is a moment in time—a destiny moment—that awakens our sensibility and summons the sleeping giant within us to arise out of a slumbering state. Every one of us will have a pigpen experience that causes the proverbial "light bulb" to be clicked on.

Each moment announces an opportunity for something new to happen. You are writing the story of your life one moment at a time. Make certain it's epic. Make it spectacular!

The philosopher Horace said, "There is a critical minute for all things." How you respond to these moments will determine the course of your life and the nature of your destiny. You can procrastinate and complain—or you can make a decision to do something different. You can be distracted and lose those momentary opportunities to change course—or focus on that upward call of God (see Phil. 3:14). Don't procrastinate any longer. Come to your self—and value your soul enough to nurture it (see Luke 15:17).

ONE STEP TOWARD RESILIENCY

Do you value yourself?

Here are some ways you can start evaluating *how* you value yourself.

- Who are your friends? Your relationships? Those you assemble with? *How do they treat you?*

- What are your dreams, visions, and aspirations? Are they small and insignificant (because you consider yourself small or insignificant), or are they bold, courageous, and big?

- How do you talk about yourself? *Are you confident and kind, or are you critical and harsh?*

Decide today that you will value your own soul so that others will start treating you appropriately.

> " *You need to value your soul more than other people value your soul.* "

Day Seven

REWRITE YOUR MENTAL SCRIPT

*Finally, brethren, whatever things are true,
whatever things are noble, whatever things are
just, whatever things are pure, whatever things are
lovely, whatever things are of good report, if there is
any virtue and if there is anything praiseworthy—
meditate on these things.* —PHILIPPIANS 4:8

Paul's criteria for a godly thought life *also* applies to the way you think about yourself. If anything, the soul should be one of the key areas to which we apply this mode of thought evaluation. Remember, Jesus invited us to love our neighbor *as we love ourselves.* We freely give *what we freely receive.* If our internal script is off and in disagreement with what God says about who we are and how we should think about ourselves, we cannot be a life-giving conduit for His love to flow through. To do this, you must be prepared to give up your childhood scripts. Those childish ways can prove to be dangerous.

More dangerous, however, is being in disagreement with God's script concerning us. When our internal scripts (and beliefs) are contrary to God's Word (and His will), we set ourselves up for failure. False scripts about who we are and what we are worth shape our mindsets, paradigms, and belief systems.

What we believe determines who we become, *"for as he thinketh in his heart, so is he"* (Prov. 23:7 KJV).

This is exactly what happened to the prodigal son. He was a son of honor, wealth, and great affluence. Yet he believed a script that joined him to some nameless citizen who sent him to feed pigs as his profession. The son could have rewritten his mental script *before* this exchange took place. However, he did not, and as a result the parable gives us a powerful warning when it comes to the thoughts we choose to think about *who we are*. If our mental script is not in agreement with God's, it becomes very easy for us to embrace what others think about us—even when what they think is clearly out of sync with our God-ordained purpose and God-assigned identity.

ONE STEP TOWARD RESILIENCY

Write down Philippians 4:8 in a prominent place where you can constantly see it (on your phone, on your mirror, refrigerator, somewhere at work, etc.).

This is your criterion for evaluating how you should think—specifically, how you should think about *yourself*!

" Change starts in our minds. "

_____

_____

_____

_____

_____

_____

WHAT WAS I THINKING?

*For the weapons of our warfare are not carnal
but mighty in God for pulling down strongholds,
casting down arguments and every high thing
that exalts itself against the knowledge of God,
bringing every thought into captivity to the
obedience of Christ.* —2 Corinthians 10:4-5

Looking back, the prodigal son should have applied this warfare principle to his unfortunate state of affairs. The enemy is after the control of your soul. When the nameless citizen proposed that the son join together with him and feed pigs, something should have provoked him to say, "I don't do pigs!" But by that time he was already living disconnected from his authentic self. He should have been aware enough to know that he was not a swine feeder and that feeding swine was a compromise of his core values—his non-negotiables. If he was really connected and cognizant of what he was doing, he certainly would not have gone around uniting himself to arbitrary people he barely even knew. The option presented by the citizen should have sounded so ridiculous that it was rejected without a second thought. Using the language of Paul, the son needed to "cast down" this proposal as something preposterous—as something in utter disagreement with his identity. *He did not* because he did not know who he was. When you don't know who you are, you don't know how to value yourself.

Consider this. The reason that we tend to reflect on old dating relationships and exclaim in disbelief, "*What was I thinking? I must have been out of my right mind!*" is because we did not seize control of our mental script. Like the prodigal, perhaps we were immature and ignorant. We were ignorant of who we truly were, and because we were not soul-aware enough we simply joined ourselves together with people who, likewise, did not see and call out the treasure within us. Changing our scripts helps us to do this.

Reflect on the thought Paul shares with the Corinthians: "*When I was a child, I spoke as a child, I understood as a child, I thought as a child; but when I became a man, I put away childish things*" (1 Cor. 13:11).

We grow up by bringing our thoughts into captivity as Paul instructs, causing them to obey Christ. This is how we must approach the thoughts and mental scripts that try to undermine our value. Paul uses violent language because the assault against our value is equally violent. Refuse to accept any message that attempts to question the precious value of your soul.

ONE STEP TOWARD RESILIENCY

Take this opportunity to ask the Holy Spirit to help you identify the thoughts that are trying to devalue your soul.

Identify these thoughts, by name, and cast them down as arguments and strongholds that exalt themselves against the knowledge of Christ.

Finally, ask the Holy Spirit for the power to rewrite new mental scripts that are in agreement with God's Word and His purpose for your life.

*We can change our lives by
changing the way we think.*

Day Nine

MOVING AHEAD OR MOVING ON?

But one thing I do, forgetting those things which
are behind and reaching forward to those things
which are ahead. —PHILIPPIANS 3:13

Remember the example of Lot, his daughters, and his wife? Lot and his daughters were able to move on, while his wife could only move ahead—she stayed connected to the past by looking back without severing the emotional attachment. When we move ahead, it becomes easy to look back.

To move on, however, is to progress beyond your past. To move on is to step into your next season. To move on is to not only physically put one foot in front of the other, but to mentally rewrite your thought patterns to agree with where God is taking you. You are a multi-dimensional being who is moving ahead in every sphere. Your body is moving. Your mind is moving. Your soul is moving.

This is where we need to pause. Your body might be walking, but your soul may still be snared by the past. Lot's wife's was. She was internally connected to her old way of life in Sodom. Even if she did not immediately look back, as we see in Scripture, the deteriorating condition of her soul would have prevented her from experiencing the resilient life that God ordained for her.

Somewhere down the line, she would have looked back. If it was not immediately, it would have been later. You see, her soul was looking back even before her head physically turned back.

Paul knew something about moving ahead and moving on. He did not pretend away his past—and neither should you. Paul agreed with the new script God was writing for him. He used the past to his advantage, to reveal the power of God to totally transform a snarling, murderous persecutor of the faith to a dynamic ambassador of the Kingdom.

ONE STEP TOWARD RESILIENCY

Are you moving ahead or moving on? Ask yourself:

- How do I think or talk about negative events and experiences in my past?
- How have I handled unforgiveness?
- Am I still holding on to hurt, or have I moved on to where yesterday's hurt and pain have become fire for my journey today?

Are you still struggling with the old script of your past, or have you decided to believe God's new script for your life...where your past no longer has an internal hold on your soul?

> *To forget means to sever something so that you can move on.*

_____

_____

_____

_____

_____

Day Ten

BECOMING SOUL-AWARE

For what profit is it to a man if he gains the whole world, and loses his own soul? Or what will a man give in exchange for his soul? —MATTHEW 16:26

I have used the phrase "soul-aware" a few times so far in our time together. This simply means that we recognize and are aware of the true value of our souls—as defined by Jesus Himself relative to our identity, personality, intelligence, giftedness, abilities, purpose, and potential. When we live aware of this value, our choices, daily decisions, and ultimately our destiny will adjust accordingly.

Mark 8:36-37 emphatically says, *"For what shall it profit a man, if he shall gain the whole world, and lose his own soul? Or what shall a man give in exchange for his soul?"* (KJV). In this text, Jesus lays the value of our soul juxtaposed against all the wealth in the world. So what is the soul of one human being really worth? The global aggregated financial/economic wealth is 233 trillion. This figure does not include, gold, silver, diamonds, uranium, plutonium, etc. that has yet to be mined or the petroleum that has not been dredged, nor any of the other commodities that have not yet been harvested, harnessed, or converted into a product, good, or consumable good. Added to this figure is all the celestial, atomic power of every star in the heavens. If you can valuate all this wealth, than you will be able to determine the value of your own soul. The enemy knows the value of your soul and so should you.

You are worth more than life can offer you because you and you alone can offer the unique gift of yourself. Be aware that the exchanges you make in life through relationships, commitments, vows, words, etc. involve your substance—*your soul.* They are not idle or unattached to you. The prodigal son surely thought he was leaving his father's house and was going to try things out on his own. He not only squandered all he had materially and financially; in the process, he lost himself.

When we believe incorrect mental scripts about who we are and the value of our souls, it becomes easier to give our personal power away to just *anyone.* Again, we see this exemplified with the prodigal son and the citizen. Any attention or perceived value that we receive from someone else (not just in a relational context, but maybe a business context), we quickly embrace. After all, our soul longs for bonding. The problem is we enter into these unions without a *second thought.* Why? We have not honestly considered the pricelessness of our soul.

Jesus asked the question in Matthew 16:26, not expecting an answer, but hoping to incite serious consideration. He wants you to become completely overwhelmed by the value He attaches to your soul. *Your* soul. Your uniqueness. The man or woman God formed and fashioned you to be. There is no price tag on this. The mere thought of something so valuable being exchanged for *anything* should make us severely unsettled. And yet many of us are making these exchanges on a regular basis.

In the days and weeks to come, we are going to specifically identify ways that you might have entered into an exchange *because* you did not correctly value the worth of your soul. Let us agree together that, through the power of the Holy Spirit, these exchanges will be identified and broken in your life, and replacing the old cycles will be an incredible, new, resilient expression of the abundant life God has for you—the hope and future God promises (Jer. 29:11).

ONE STEP TOWARD RESILIENCY

Try to identify one exchange that you have made and feel currently bound by because you did not properly value yourself. *Write this down.*

If you are still cloudy on what these exchanges look like, we will study them in greater detail in the weeks to come.

In the meantime, ask the Holy Spirit for wisdom to recognize any and all exchanges you have made because you did not appropriately value your soul. Also, ask Him to make you aware of any soul ties you are currently bound by that need to be broken.

" You cannot put a price tag on your soul. "

WHAT HAPPENS WHEN YOU LOSE TOUCH WITH YOUR SOUL?

He restores my soul. —PSALMS 23:3

Your spirit makes you God conscious.
Your body makes you world conscious.
Your soul makes you self-conscious.

SUMMARY

You do not lose your soul like a set of car keys or a pair of socks in the dryer. Nor is the process likened to the age-old transaction of "selling your soul to the devil," where you sign on the dotted line and now live out an irrevocable contract. These are lies the enemy tries to tell you in order to keep you trapped in a cycle of bondage.

To *lose your soul* would be more accurately defined as "losing *touch* with your soul." When the prodigal son joined himself to a citizen of the country, he did not literally give away his soul. Rather, he became so detached from the truth of who he really was that it was almost like he was giving his soul away.

Once you appropriately begin to value your soul, it becomes very important for you to take inventory. In this session, you discover that your soul has a minimum of seven desires or longings. If these are not being satisfied internally, you will look for ways to silence their cry *externally*.

The deep desires of the human soul were always meant to be satisfied in communion with God. No one understands us more intimately than our heavenly Father, as He created and formed us each individually—nor does anyone value the health of our souls more. Nurturing that relationship is what it means to satisfy our soul longings *internally*. If this healthy exchange with God is not taking place, we start to look *externally*—to other people, habits, paradigms, cultures, businesses, etc. Even good people and healthy things can become a deadly soul attachment if we allow them to replace or overshadow our relationship with God.

LEARN

Watch Session 3 of the *Reclaim Your Soul* video series.

Discuss

Engage your group in conversation using the following questions.

1. How is your soul different from your spirit? (Can you explain the difference between body, soul, and spirit?)

2. What are some of the things that happen in our lives when we give our souls away? Dr. Trimm listed nine things.

3. What attributes and characteristics of the soul were surprising to you?

4. Explain the following statement: "You cannot give God glory until you fully express who you are."

5. Can you list some examples in Scripture of people whom God called and yet, at the time of their calling, they did not know who they were (so God had to remind them)?

6. Has God ever called you to accomplish something that seemed impossible? If so, what kind of encouragement did He give you and how did this change your thinking?

7. List and discuss the seven desires of the soul.

8. Why is it so important that these desires are satisfied in a healthy way (with God)?

EMPOWER

Choose one of the "seven desires of the soul."

Your task: Identify *practical, everyday* ways that you can satisfy that specific desire of the soul in God.

It is one thing to talk about this as a concept. However, this exercise is designed to make this very practical and, from each group member's experience, share strategies on how to satisfy the longings of our soul in God (thus avoiding soul ties and attachments).

SUSTAIN

This week, for about five minutes each day, you will be focusing on specific Scripture verses for daily reflection and meditation.

Day Eleven

DESIGNED FOR WORSHIP

*Bless the Lord, O my soul; and all that is within
me, bless His holy name!* —PSALMS 103:1

Your soul was created by God, for God (see Col. 1:16; Gen. 2:7). It finds ultimate expression in giving Him the worship that is due Him. Later on in the week, we will discuss how your uniqueness offers up glory to God. For now, I want you to understand that you were created for worship. Your soul was designed to both give *and* be an offering to God.

One of the areas of our minds that needs to be renewed is what worship looks like. Worship is not just something that takes place during the music portion of a church service; worship is when your entire being responds to God. This includes your soul.

Scripture is full of directives for the soul to worship God. Your soul being connected with God through worship is absolutely essential if it is going to be truly satisfied, as it cannot find meaning, purpose, and ultimately satisfaction apart from its Maker.

Conversely, if you lose your soul and become disconnected from who you are, it becomes difficult for you to give worship. This is where so many slip into religion, for one shade of religion

Reclaim *Your Soul* STUDY GUIDE

is when a person has lost their authentic grasp of self and simply follows a system, assuming that the system is sufficient for worship. Religious systems are incompatible with worship when the system replaces the soul. Remember, a system cannot offer God what only your soul can.

God is seeking those who worship in spirit and truth. One dimension of worshiping in truth involves the worshiper's authenticity. This does not mean the worshiper is perfect. It does not mean they are flawless or without fault. Authentic worship flows from a worshiper who embraces who they are in Christ—who is perfectly satisfied and in love with the reflection of His love they were created to reveal.

ONE STEP TOWARD RESILIENCY

Assess your worship. *Who is worshiping God?* Ask yourself this one key question:

Am I worshiping God with all of my heart, soul, mind, and strength, or am I simply adhering to a religious system thinking that the system is enough? (Such as going to church services, reading the Bible, praying out of routine, etc.)

Ask the Holy Spirit to help you sort through this. If you discover that the true you is not worshiping God, break your soul tie with the system of religion and decide that *all* of you is going to respond to *all* of God in worship.

> *Worship is when we become soul-aware—*
> *it's the soul that gives God glory.*

_____

_____

_____

_____

58

Day Twelve

SAVE YOUR SOUL

Receive with meekness the implanted word, which is able to save your souls. —JAMES 1:21

Your spirit is saved and born again. Of course, this happens by grace through faith, with the process being initiated by the Spirit of God. What we read about in the first chapter of James is something quite different.

In his epistle, James gives us practical instruction on how to save—or protect—our souls.

He informs us that our soul is saved through the "implanted word." This means that Scripture is key in protecting us from giving our souls away and thus surrendering our personal power.

The Word of God is your constant affirmation source, reminding your soul of who you truly are. Your mind, your will, and your emotions are not instantly saved upon your conversion. Though your spirit is saved, immediately quickened by the Holy Spirit, and set apart for Heaven when you are born again, every other dimension of who you are is launched into a glorious lifelong process. This is what James is talking about here. Your life embarks upon the journey of becoming conformed into the image of Jesus Christ. Ultimately, this involves what took place in your spirit impacting every other dimension of your being—starting with your soul.

Your feet will only travel where your mind can take you. Your mind is an expression of your soul. In other words, your physical body will adjust based on what first takes place in the soul realm. So how is our soul "saved"? How do you know how you should think? Behave? Respond? The Word of God is your source for daily living, giving your soul a vital blueprint on how to move toward Christlikeness.

ONE STEP TOWARD RESILIENCY

Do you have a daily Bible reading program? If not, I encourage you to begin one.

- *Do not* overcomplicate this. Start simple. If it is one chapter a day, great.

- If it's going through a daily devotional book where you think about *one* specific verse each day—excellent.

- Start with something. Five minutes, ten minutes, twenty minutes. Quality always trumps quantity.

Start somewhere and recognize that what you read *feeds* your soul, providing a blueprint for how you think, behave, and live.

> *The Word of God is your divine blueprint for building a healthy soul.*

_____

_____

_____

_____

Day Thirteen

SOUL DESIRES

*Delight yourself also in the Lord, and He shall give
you the desires of your heart.* —PSALMS 37:4

We lose our souls when we set out on the wrong journey to satisfy the seven soul longings—to bond, grow, know, be known, acquire, accomplish, achieve significance, and feel safe. The wrong journey is the external one (versus the internal one). The external journey seeks to fulfill the seven desires of our soul in people, places, things, opportunities, etc. This is what causes us to lose ourselves and enter into a soul attachment. God told Abraham to disconnect from everything that would keep him anchored to his past. He maintained one soul tie, which he was later challenged to sever. Then he was able to see his future from God's perspective. Until that moment, he was "blinded" to the great life ahead of him (see Gen. 12:1-8).

When we submit our own life journey before the Maker of our soul—the author and finisher of our faith who promised to complete the good work He began in each of us—we approach the only One able to answer our questions, satisfy our longings, maximize our potential, and fulfill the desires of our soul (see Heb. 12:2; Phil. 1:6).

Consider this. God does not awaken desires within you that He does not intend or is unable to fulfill Himself. Appetite is God's assurance that what your soul longs for can be experienced. Again, the key is satisfying the longings of your soul in God, and God alone.

In Isaiah 58:11, we see that *"the Lord will guide you continually, and satisfy your soul in drought, and strengthen your bones; you shall be like a watered garden, and like a spring of water, whose waters do not fail."*

ONE STEP TOWARD RESILIENCY

Reflect on the seven longings of the soul. They are:

1. To bond

2. To grow

3. To know

4. To be known

5. To acquire

6. To achieve significance

7. To feel safe

Which one(s) of these seven longings is a driving force in your life? Take time to thoughtfully consider your answer. Perhaps you are looking to fulfill this soul desire through a relationship, career change, or major purchase (such as a house or a car). Remember, even good things cannot ultimately satisfy those deep longings of your soul.

Bring whatever desire or longing you've identified to the One who satisfies your soul, the Lord, and ask Him to begin satisfying that soul longing.

> *God doesn't give you desires unless He expects those desires to come to pass.*

Day Fourteen

GIVING GOD GLORY

For You have made him a little lower than
the angels, and You have crowned him
with glory and honor. —PSALMS 8:5

In this majestic psalm of David, he writes about the measure of glory that God the Creator has conferred upon man, His creation. We cannot overlook this or bypass it as insignificant. You must know that God created *you* with glory and honor.

This concept can seem intimidating to people. After all, the last thing we want to do is rob God of glory. However, consider that when you *receive* glory, you *have* glory to give. When you function in your divine design and created capacity, you exude the glory that God Himself conferred upon you. Too many of us push our *selves* aside, buying into the lie that our humanity is evil. If humanity is evil, then somewhere along the line, God made a tragic mistake in creating us *human*. Sin is evil, not humanity. Sin corrupted the beautiful work that was and is humanity. The worst thing we can do is directly associate our humanity with sin. Often, we include our soul in the humanity package, because the soul animates our humanity. As a result, we devalue ourselves. We think, "Self is evil." The soul is corrupt and thus not worth hanging on to. This is what makes us vulnerable to soul ties and unhealthy emotional attachments.

When our soul is not giving God the glory that it was designed to, it will give itself to other things, people, and attachments. You cannot give God glory when you've already given your own glory away—you'll have nothing left to give.

You were created in the image and likeness of God. You were fashioned uniquely. When you function according to the way you were designed, the expression of your uniqueness and individuality actually gives God glory.

The sun gives glory when it functions in alignment with its divine design. If the sun stopped shining, it would not give the Creator glory. Likewise, you give God glory when you fully express yourself. This is why this topic of "losing your soul" is so concerning.

ONE STEP TOWARD RESILIENCY

What do you think about your humanity?

Take this opportunity to ask the Holy Spirit to help you identify how you see your humanity—your soul—who you are.

If you find yourself thinking negatively about your humanity, believing it to be directly associated with sin, ask the Lord to change the way you think and empower you to fully express who you were created to be in order to give Him the glory that He deserves.

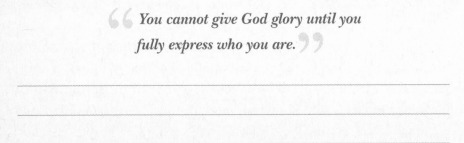

You cannot give God glory until you fully express who you are.

_____

_____

_____

Day Fifteen

OUT OF CONTEXT

*But when the desire comes, it is a tree
of life.* —PROVERBS 13:12

If the desire of our souls is not being satisfied in a healthy context, we will gravitate toward unhealthy soul ties and attachments. We cannot look externally for that which can only be satisfied internally.

In the process of searching for soul satisfaction, we will look for anybody or anything that promises to fulfill any of the seven desires of the soul. We see this clearly exemplified in the prodigal son, who, in the process of losing his soul, became willing to join himself to a stranger and feed pigs.

People, programs, and even products will claim they can satisfy these longings; they cannot. Business opportunities or careers may appear hopeful, but in the end they will fall short. Entertainment. Travel. Education. All sorts of good things will *appear* to fulfill these longings, but they will consistently fail.

It would make perfect sense that the only One capable of fulfilling your soul is the One who formed and fashioned it to begin with. There is none who is more intimately acquainted with the true you than your wonderful Maker.

The pursuit of fulfilling the desires of your heart is correct and healthy. It becomes problematic and dangerous when the concept is approached *out of context*—outside of God. Remember, it is when we delight ourselves in Him that He gives us the desires of our heart (see Ps. 27:4; 21:2). Desires rooted in a purpose outside of delighting in the Lord will make us vulnerable to ungodly soul ties.

One Step toward Resiliency

Where are the desires of your heart currently being satisfied?

- Relationships
- Family
- Success
- Career
- Education
- Money

By answering this question, you will understand the context in which you are attempting to fulfill your soul's longings.

If the context is not God, go to Him now as the one true Source of fulfillment. This one decision can change everything!

> " *We cannot look externally for what can only be satisfied internally.* "

_____

_____

_____

_____

_____

Session Four

IDENTIFYING SOUL TIES AND ATTACHMENTS

*Then he went and joined himself to a
citizen of that country.* —LUKE 15:15

*You can be saved and on your way to Heaven, but live
in bondage during your time on Earth
because of who or what you are attached to.*

SUMMARY

In order to break soul ties and attachments, it is very important you first know how to identify them.

For many believers, the term "soul tie" is completely foreign. Then, for those who are familiar with the language, the definition tends to be narrow. A soul tie would be defined as something that exclusively takes place in the context of a relationship—often a romantic one.

As you will discover in this session (and note in the *Reclaim Your Soul* book), soul ties and attachments are more frequent than we imagine and they take place is multiple contexts—romantic relationships being only one expression of these exchanges.

What makes a soul tie dangerous is not the concept; it is the context. There are legitimate, healthy soul ties. The key is being able to distinguish what is healthy from what is dysfunctional—what is life enhancing from life depleting. This is the goal of this session—to help you identify what soul ties are, distinguish positive soul ties from negative ones, and recognize the presence of any negative soul attachments in your life. This is the first step to freedom. Remember, you cannot confront what you do not recognize is there.

LEARN

Watch Session 4 of the *Reclaim Your Soul* video series.

DISCUSS

Engage your group in conversation using the following questions.

1. How have you thought about soul ties/soul attachments in the past? (Were they strictly relational? Or have you never even heard of such a thing as soul ties?)

2. Why do you think some of the strongest soul tries are created through sexual relations and addiction?

3. What happens when we don't know the value of our own soul? How does this push us toward creating soul ties in our lives?

4. Why is it important to "qualify" people before you join yourself to them in close relationship?

5. Are there actually legitimate soul ties? List some examples of healthy soul ties.

6. How can soul ties create problems?

7. How does becoming conscious of soul ties begin our journey to breaking them?

8. Why do you think spiritual soul ties might be some of the most dangerous?

EMPOWER

Your leader will be dividing the room into seven groups and assign each group one of the seven soul tie categories.

Based on what you watched in the video, make a list of at least five soul ties or attachments that could fall under your group's assigned soul tie category.

At the end, everyone will come together and share what they wrote down.

SUSTAIN

This week, for about five minutes each day, you will be focusing on specific Scripture verses for daily reflection and meditation.

Day Sixteen

SETUP FOR SOUL TIES

Then he went and joined himself to a
citizen of that country. —LUKE 15:15

We enter into destructive soul ties and attachments when we illegitimately try to satisfy the legitimate desires of the soul. These are the seven desires that we reviewed earlier in our study. They are meant to be satisfied internally, not externally. God is the One who helps us navigate these desires. When we begin looking outside of that context for soul satisfaction, it becomes easy to join ourselves to people, experiences, or situations that form soul ties.

The prodigal son is the perfect example of this. He refused to look internally because he believed an incorrect script. The only one who could help him rediscover himself and reclaim his soul was his father. Sadly, the son expected condemnation and rejection from his father and so he looked externally for other solutions. How the son viewed his father is how so many incorrectly view the heavenly Father.

Believing false scripts is one of the key factors that makes us vulnerable to soul ties. As a result of what the son believed about his father, he joined himself with someone who did not know him at all nor cared to know him. The citizen of the country was not concerned about the state of the boy's soul or how to help him recover his true identity. This citizen had a selfish agenda and wanted to use the son for his own purpose—feeding his pigs. Those on the other side of dangerous soul ties are not interested in you fulfilling your potential, but they want to use you to promote their own agendas. When you boldly go to the Father and ask Him to satisfy the longings of your soul, you will receive the affirmation and acceptance you need to destroy any notion that you are not enough just as you are.

ONE STEP TOWARD RESILIENCY

What do you believe about God the Father?

Is He mad, angry, and condemning, or is He a good God who lavishes unconditional love upon His children?

How you see God is vital in determining whether or not you enter into a destructive soul tie.

If you believe that God is angry and upset with you, you will look for relationships or experiences that bring condemnation.

If you believe God is good and loves you unconditionally, you will approach Him with confidence, asking Him to satisfy the desires of your soul.

God is good, and He invites you to come before Him boldly. His is a throne of grace and mercy. He accepts you because of what Jesus did on your behalf. Approach His presence today and ask Him to satisfy the longings of your soul.

> *We enter destructive soul ties and attachments when we illegitimately try to satisfy the legitimate desires of our soul.*

Day Seventeen

CHRISTIANS CAN HAVE SOUL TIES

Do you not know that your bodies are members of
Christ? Shall I then take the members of Christ and
make them members of a harlot? Certainly not! Or
do you not know that he who is joined to a harlot
is one body with her? For "the two," He says, "shall
become one flesh." —1 CORINTHIANS 6:15-16

You can be saved, but enslaved. While this is a disheartening reality, it is nevertheless a fact that countless believers struggle with every single day of their lives. The first thing one must recognize is that yes, it is possible to be a Christian—to be born again and on your way to Heaven—but to live a lifestyle of bondage on earth because of soul ties.

Consider this about the prodigal son. His identity never changed in his father's sight. He went off, did his own thing, and yes, even forgot who he was. Regardless, he remained his father's son. You can be a child of God but still forget who you are, and as a result fall prey to soul ties. The boy's mere identity as a son did not safeguard him from forming a soul tie with the citizen we spoke of earlier. Likewise, your identity as a Christian does not keep you from entering into an unhealthy soul attachment.

The story of the prodigal son is a story of identity. When Adam fell, he fell from a place of being fully conscious of who he was—his true identity. He fell into the realm of sin. Sin caused humanity's operating system to crash. Grace pushed the reset button. Grace gives us a complete spiritual overhaul of our operating system—how we function as human beings.

The prodigal son is a story of someone falling from grace and descending into sin. But where sin abounds, grace much more abounds. Even in your weakest moment, grace will cover you!

When Adam fell, he suffered from spiritual amnesia—generation after generation we have lost the true meaning of what it means to be human. We now view being human as being flawed, but grace takes us from being flawed to being fabulous!

> *To be human has been associated with being flawed. But when God created us, he did not create us to be flawed, but fabulous.*

Believe that you are fabulous just as you are—and live as though it is true! We need to live in agreement with our true, God-given identity. The problem is too many Christians forget who they are and as a result join themselves to anyone or anything that makes them "feel" affirmed, thus forming life-draining, self-destructive, destiny-sabotaging soul ties.

One Step toward Resiliency

Do you know who you really are?

I am not talking about your ability to simply quote some Christian jargon. Do you actually believe that you are a son or daughter of Royalty—once more, are you living as if this is *true?*

You can evaluate this by assessing the level of freedom you are presently walking in. If you sense the presence of a soul tie in your life, that means you are not living in agreement with what is true about your identity in Christ.

Christians are not exempt from soul attachments and the resulting consequences. The realities concerning your identity in Christ, however, should help you guard your soul from any such attachments. Remembering your true identity—who and whose you are—is the best way to vaccinate your soul.

> *Start living like you actually are everything*
> *that God says that you are.*

DEFINE SOUL TIES

*Christ has set us free to live a free life. So take
your stand! Never again let anyone put a harness
of slavery on you.*—GALATIANS 5:1, MSG

In Galatians 5:1, the apostle Paul clearly communicates the heart
of God concerning bondage—it is *not* His will. In context, Paul
is discussing the enslaving power of law and religious protocol,
but the heart of the issue is what those things produce—putting
free people in bondage. As a believer, it is not God's will for you
to live in bondage to anyone or anything, for this evidences a *free*
man or woman living in disagreement with what Jesus paid for
on the cross. Soul ties are shackles that keep us in this place of
bondage. The key is identifying what they are so we are able to
confront and break them.

One clear definition of a soul tie would be as follows: The
emotional, spiritual, and psychological attachments to things,
people, and experiences that, at a subconscious level, influence
the decisions we make in life.

Right from the beginning, I want you to know that soul ties
or soul attachments (the terms are interchangeable) are *far more*
than just relational, in terms of person-to-person exchanges. This
is only one dimension of how soul ties are made. The problem

is we may be familiar with the language of "soul ties" but unfamiliar with how many different ways these attachments can be created in our lives. This has been the goal of this study—in particular, this week's session and corresponding exercises.

There are at least seven different categories of soul ties. We covered them in our video session, but just for review's sake, they are: 1) spiritual, 2) intellectual, 3) professional, 4) social, 5) emotional, 6) physical, and 7) institutional. The book *Reclaim Your Soul* breaks these down in tremendous detail while equipping you with the forty disciplines that will help you make new exchanges in your life—replacing the old exchanges that gave birth to these bondage-inducing soul ties.

ONE STEP TOWARD RESILIENCY

How free are you currently living?

Would your life be defined by freedom in Christ, or would it be described as bound—to people, addictions, behaviors, etc.?

The goal in asking this question is not to provoke condemnation but to initiate healing. In order to heal, our true state must first be revealed.

If you are in bondage to anyone or anything, take heart—*bondage is not God's will for your life* and He wants you to experience the freedom that Jesus died to give you! It's not enough to know "freedom" as a concept or theology; God wants you to live it out every single day of your life. Commit to opening your heart to the Holy Spirit's work and honestly yielding to the process in the days ahead.

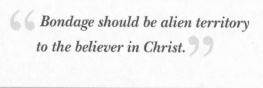

Bondage should be alien territory to the believer in Christ.

IDENTIFY YOUR SOUL TIES

*Therefore if the Son makes you free, you
shall be free indeed.* —JOHN 8:36

This is where we need to get real, open, and authentic. The idea of having some type of "soul tie" in our lives may sound awful, but everyone, at some point or another, deals with these different attachments. This is a journey not meant for you to "beware," but rather be "aware."

Be encouraged, your status before God is secure. You are His child. He does not look upon you as some second-rate person because you are dealing with soul ties—it is the human condition. Remember yesterday's entry? God wants you *free.* He doesn't want you feeling condemned. He doesn't want to rub your face in your mistake or bondage or bad choice. This is not His heart and is contrary to how He operates. It bears repeating that Scripture makes it clear that "*if the Son liberates you [makes you free men], then you are really and unquestionably free*" (John 8:36 AMP). This study is about incorporating this foundational truth into your lifestyle.

The first step to walking in freedom is *asking the Holy Spirit to help you recognize areas of bondage.* Too many of us avoid this step because of the hurt or pain we perceive it will cause. The greatest pain is not in the confrontation of bondage but rather the maintenance of bondage. Many continue to live trapped in the cycle of bondage simply because they are unwilling to confront and acknowledge what they already know to be true.

God absolutely respects your vulnerability and will not exploit it. Religion exploits. People exploit. The enemy exploits—he will attempt to flood your mind with condemnation. But when you invite the Holy Spirit in and ask Him to help you recognize the exchanges that have created bondages in your life, He comes to bring truth with one purpose—your complete freedom. The Holy Spirit is your advisor and advocate! Religion is about what you can *give to* God. Salvation is about what God *gives you*. Religion is about what you can do *for God*. Salvation is about what God can do *for you*.

ONE STEP TOWARD RESILIENCY

Boldly ask the Holy Spirit to help you identify the soul ties in your life. Spend some time in silent prayer. As certain areas of bondage or specific attachments enter your mind, *write them down*. These will be your targets for the remaining four weeks of the study.

Pray the prayer that David prayed in Psalm 51.

> *Oh, give me back my joy again; you have broken me— now let me rejoice.*
>
> *Don't keep looking at my sins. Remove the stain of my guilt.*
>
> *Create in me a clean heart, O God. Renew a loyal spirit within me.*
>
> *Do not banish me from your presence, and don't take your Holy Spirit from me.*
>
> *Restore to me the joy of your salvation, and make me willing to obey you.*
>
> *Then I will teach your ways to rebels, and they will return to you.*

Forgive me for shedding blood, O God who saves; then I will joyfully sing of your forgiveness.

Unseal my lips, O Lord, that my mouth may praise you.

You do not desire a sacrifice, or I would offer one. You do not want a burnt offering.

The sacrifice you desire is a broken spirit. You will not reject a broken and repentant heart, O God.

Look with favor on Zion and help her; rebuild the walls of Jerusalem.

Then you will be pleased with sacrifices offered in the right spirit—with burnt offerings and whole burnt offerings (Psalms 51:8-19 NLT).

Know that God wants you to be free from every bondage and attachment more than you want to be free!

> **Our greatest pain should not be confronting our bondage, but in maintaining it.**

_____

_____

_____

_____

_____

_____

_____

_____

_____

Day Twenty

YOUR NEXT STEP

And you shall know the truth, and the truth shall make you free. —JOHN 8:32

There are four weeks left in this study. In our remaining time together, we are going to study some practical ways to walk in freedom and liberty. However, to experience results with this course, it is absolutely critical that you embrace how important this journey really is. Your next steps will be governed and determined by your perspective. Your perspective will guide your choices, and your choices will determine your destiny. It really is *that* simple.

Many people never move into the *next step* because they: 1) overcomplicate the process, 2) want to avoid a potential discomfort, or 3) prefer a more experience-based temporary solution. In other words, we would rather visit the altar every week at a church/event and have a pastor or leader pray for us. We mistakenly believe that we can live our Christian lives riding on the wings of a prayer that someone else prayed over us. Those prayers are catalysts designed to initiate a *process*, not become an "end all" solution.

Are there instances where a single prayer brings complete deliverance and freedom? Absolutely. There are many, as this is the essence of a *miracle*. The problem is the enemy is not concerned about someone who receives freedom; he is terrified of the believer who sustains freedom as a lifestyle. In other words, he knows that if we think of freedom as an experience or one-time answer to prayer, then he can come back with some new form of bondage causing us to go through the entire cycle again.

I want to help you break the cycle *and* establish a new way of resilient living. Will the enemy come against you? Yes, but his tactics cannot prevail against anyone submitted to God (see James 4:7). He will try, but fail. Why? Because you decided to agree with the truth that God wants you to live free as a lifestyle (see Gal. 5:1)—and this truth is what sets you free *every day of your life!*

ONE STEP TOWARD RESILIENCY

What truth do you need to confront in order to take a step toward a freer lifestyle?

Have you had people pray for you while neglecting the practical steps necessary to sustaining freedom in your life? Hebrews 12:1-2 states you must *"lay aside every weight, and the sin which so easily ensnares us."*

Are you holding off on dealing with some "truth" in your life because you think that it will be too painful to deal with?

Settle in your heart and mind today that *no matter how you feel* you will confront the truth.

> *Your perspective will guide your choices, and your choices will determine your destiny.*

_____

_____

_____

_____

KEYS TO CONFRONTING DYSFUNCTIONAL RELATIONSHIPS

*The righteous should choose his friends
carefully, for the way of the wicked leads
them astray.* —PROVERBS 12:26

*When you change the way you look at
things, circumstances, and people...things,
circumstances, and people change the way
they look. It's all about perspective.*

SUMMARY

One principle that remains consistent throughout *Reclaim Your Soul* is the idea that you resemble those with whom you assemble. If you want to change your life, you may need to change your company. Could things be the way they are because you are the way you are? What one thing can you change that could change everything?

You can change the way you see yourself. Changing the way you see yourself will change the way you value yourself.

People don't just show up in your life. You make a conscious choice as to whether or not you allow them entry into your relationship circle. They may try to convince you that friendship with them is without option—acting like it is mandated—when the reality is *you always have options* when it comes to your relationships.

In this session, you will learn how to identify dysfunctional relationships through dysfunctional attributes and characteristics. Once you recognize dysfunction, you are able to confront it. Dr. Trimm equips you with seven keys that will put you back in control when it comes to whom you allow into your life.

Relationships lift you up or tear you down. You need people around you who will take you to the next level rather than keep you trapped where you are. Want to change your life? Change your relationships.

LEARN

Watch Session 5 of the *Reclaim Your Soul* video series.

DISCUSS

Engage your group in conversation using the following questions.

1. What image comes to your mind when you think of dysfunctional relationships?

2. Why is it so important to have a clear definition of dysfunction?

3. What happens when we mistakenly think the relationships we are in are *not* dysfunctional (when in fact they are—we just don't have a clear definition of "dysfunctional")?

4. How can dysfunctional relationships be with more than just people?

5. In what ways do people tolerate dysfunction in their lives and relationships?

6. What are some of the reasons for holding on to dysfunctional relationships?

7. Discuss the seven keys to confronting dysfunctional relationships. If time permits, have seven people in the group discuss one of the keys that impacted them most.

8. How can we change how other people look at us?

9. What does a "next-level lifting" relationship look like (based on Mark 2:1-3)?

Empower

Make a relationship list, writing down the people you: 1) are closest to, and 2) spend the most time with. This should include family, friends, and coworkers. Please use specific names in the following categories:

1. Circle of trust

2. Intimate relationships

3. Friends

4. Colleagues

5. Strangers

6. Enemies

After the list is constructed, prayerfully evaluate each relationship and ask, "How is this relationship a reflection of *myself*?"

Remind yourself that this is not cause for condemnation, separation, judgment, or comparison. This is a call to examine why you have the types of relationships you do by identifying specific characteristics within your own self.

You cannot change anyone but your own self. You may have criteria for all of your relationships—especially your most inner circles of trust—but at the end of the day, change starts from within. Things are the way they are because you are the way you are.

Sustain

This week, for about five minutes each day, you will be focusing on specific Scripture verses for daily reflection and meditation.

Day Twenty-One

YOUR RELATIONSHIPS REVEAL YOU

Can two walk together, unless they
are agreed? —AMOS 3:3

This is an incredible verse, as it cuts right to the heart of the matter and challenges us about *our* role and responsibility in maintaining dysfunctional relationships. We don't just *fall* into relationships. There is mutuality. There is agreement. There is a common bond between two people—even if the bond is one of dysfunction.

Even though we know that bad company corrupts good character, could it also be possible that we are drawn to bad company because, somewhere inside of us, there is some character shaping that needs to take place? In other words, we allow these individuals in our lives because they reflect the dysfunction that is secretly hidden within ourselves, but we have never been challenged to address it. Maybe the so-called bad company connects with something unhealthy and dysfunctional inside of our selves. Throughout this study, we will continue to meditate on the fact that we assemble with those whom we resemble.

The more we focus on "the other person/people" who allegedly corrupted us or contaminated our character, we continue to give that person or group our personal power.

Responsibility is your key to reclaiming your soul. We will never begin the process unless we first own up to the fact that maybe, just maybe, we sought out the dysfunctional relationships because of the dysfunction inside of us. Such was clearly the case with the prodigal son. He was in a dysfunctional state (the impairment of healthy functioning, behavior, and attitude contrary to norms of socially acceptable and age-appropriate behavior), and as a result he entered into a dysfunctional relationship with the citizen of the country.

Taking responsibility is *not* being called into guilt, condemnation, or shame. By owning up to your participation in a dysfunctional relationship, you are making an essential and powerful move toward freedom that will begin to redesign your life completely.

ONE STEP TOWARD RESILIENCY

Take responsibility. Examine your "dysfunctional relationships" and ask yourself: "What is the commonality or agreement that we share?"

This place of agreement in a dysfunctional relationship is what must be targeted, as that is the negative bond that is keeping you attached to an unhealthy relationship.

Identity the unhealthy common bond you have with another person, repent for walking in agreement with the dysfunction, and break the tie in Jesus' Name!

This marks the beginning of restoration and health in your relationships!

> *There is a common bond between two people—*
> *even if the bond is one of dysfunction.*

Day Twenty-Two

YOU CAN SAY "NO" TO DYSFUNCTION

Make no friendship with a man given to anger, nor go with a wrathful man, lest you learn his ways and entangle yourself in a snare. —PROVERBS 22:24-25, ESV

You have control over your relationships! While you cannot control or change a person, *you* do have authority over who you allow into your life. Never let anyone try to convince you otherwise. You know someone is trying to bring you into a soul tie when they try to deceive you out of options. You always have options. You can either say "Yes" or you can say "No." The person who attempts to convince you that you *must* relate with them on a certain level or in a particular way is infringing on your personal power, and that is a major red flag.

This Scripture reminds you, loud and clear, that you have a choice. You can either make a friendship or *not* make a friendship. Relationships don't *just happen*. They are the product of mutual participation; that's why the Bible is replete with instructions on how to build healthy relationships.

If you notice dysfunction in a potential relationship, follow the author's orders and "make no friendship" with such a person. Just because someone is drawn to you and wants a relationship with you does not obligate you to participate. However, if you are already in a relationship where dysfunction abounds, I encourage you to pull away. If it is a family or spousal relationship, establish appropriate boundaries (which we will explore in greater detail later).

Never let anyone rob you of making your own destiny decisions. You have the power to choose your relationships, maintain clear boundaries, and say "No" when necessary.

ONE STEP TOWARD RESILIENCY

Remember, you always have options.

Are there people in your life right now who are trying to either 1) enter a relationship with you or 2) develop a deeper relationship with you?

If so, evaluate the level of dysfunction this person exhibits. While we are all flawed and have issues, there are clearly individuals who carry higher levels of dysfunction than others, and rather than build you up, you know the relationship would tear you down.

Remember, you have the ability to say "No." You have the power to build boundaries around your life, protecting you from entering a destructive relationship. You *always* have options.

> **Take control of the only person you
> have dominion over—yourself!**

NEXT LEVEL SEERS

*Then they came to Him, bringing a paralytic
who was carried by four men.* —MARK 2:3

While dysfunctional relationships bring you down and steer you away from fulfilling purpose, healthy friendships lift you up and move you forward. This begins in the place of seeing. How do your closest relationships *see* you? Do they have spiritual eyes that actually see through your imperfections and lock on to the potential and purpose God has wired inside of you—just waiting for the right conditions, for the right character, and yes, for the right companions to call it forth?

This is powerfully exemplified in Mark 2, where four men carry their paralyzed friend to Jesus. Unfortunately, the house where Jesus is speaking and ministering is so crowded that they cannot make it inside to see Him. They experience resistance. However, they are intent on taking their paralyzed friend into his destiny. They clearly see what is on the inside of this man. While the world looks at him and sees someone who is paralyzed, these four friends see one who is full of potential.

Do your friends see you as you *are* now or as God has called you to become? Do they treat you as paralyzed by dysfunction (like themselves) or powerful? This is a key question in evaluating healthy versus dysfunctional relationships. Dysfunctional people rarely see the gold in others; if anything, they continue to see and in turn speak to the dysfunction in their friends. Why? They can only see in others what they see in themselves. They can only summon as far as they can see. They cannot summon your greatness if they cannot see your greatness, and they cannot see your greatness if they live trapped in dysfunction.

ONE STEP TOWARD RESILIENCY

Do you feel continually encouraged to walk in your purpose and calling?

If not, ask yourself: *Do my friends see the person God created me to be, or are they in agreement with the issues, problems, and works already in progress in my life?*

This is not a call to deny reality. We are all works in progress, with God building us into the people He designed us to be through Christ. However, a key component to being who God has called us to be is surrounding ourselves with people who *see* who we are called to *become*.

This should be another non-negotiable in building the criteria for the people you allow to speak into your life and influence you.

> *People summon only as far as they can see. If your friends are not calling forth your divine destiny and purpose, they don't have eyes trained to see these realities.*

_____

_____

_____

_____

Day Twenty-Four

NEXT LEVEL LIFTERS

And when they could not come near Him
because of the crowd, they uncovered the
roof where He was. —MARK 2:4

When people see your potential, they are able to uncover the person God has created you to become. This is the next event we see happen in the story of the four men with their paralyzed friend. The man clearly had a physical barrier preventing him from walking in the fullness God had for him. Although they were turned away from the house where Jesus ministered, these four men did not give up. Their vision was tightly locked on a reality where their paralyzed friend's potential would become unleashed through a touch from the Master.

As a result, the four friends saw past the barrier and summoned the paralytic's true purpose. This type of sight produces action. In other words, when we see people as God sees them and speak to their potential, to their destiny, to their capabilities, to their purpose, and to their giftings, our actions will follow our sight. We respond according to what we see, whether in the natural or in the spirit.

It takes friends who see beyond our natural limitations and boundaries—who are able to call us up higher and bring us into the next level. This is exactly what happened with the four men and their paralyzed friend. Because they saw past the barriers, they lifted their friend up on top of the house, broke through the roof, and lowered him down in order to encounter Jesus. Because of these four friends, a paralytic walked away from that crowded house healed and whole!

ONE STEP TOWARD RESILIENCY

How are your friends building you up and lifting you higher?

Revisit the list of your friends and close companions. Next to their names write down some clear ways that their words and actions have contributed to *you* going to the next level in your life—either maximizing or minimizing your potential.

Be honest. If you find that some of these people have little or nothing to add to you in this respect, pray about the place of influence they should have in your life; if necessary, consider changing it. Remember, you have control over the relationships you invest in!

> *When people see who you truly are,*
> *they are able to build you up to be the person*
> *God has created you to be.*

_____

_____

_____

_____

_____

_____

Day Twenty-Five

SOUL MATES AND JOURNEYING COMPANIONS

*The soul of Jonathan was knit to the soul
of David, and Jonathan loved him as
his own soul.* —1 SAMUEL 18:1

As we have briefly noticed, there are also *healthy* soul ties and attachments. What exists in darkness is not original; it is simply a counterfeit of the light. Soul ties in the context of dysfunctional relationships are dangerous. When in the context of healthy relationships, however, soul ties would be described as "soul mates." Therefore, not all soul ties are bad.

One of the clearest examples of this type of relationship is pictured in First Samuel 18:1. Here we see the souls of David and Jonathan being knit together. Again, in the wrong context, this could prove disastrous and deadly. However, a soul tie in and of itself is not inherently dangerous. It is the dark counterfeit that becomes negative and unhealthy.

With David and Jonathan, we see a healthy soul attachment taking place between two close friends. Jonathan constantly reminded David of his kingly anointing, thus demonstrating that he saw and spoke over his friend accordingly. He did not agree with the threats and intimidation being doled out by his father, Saul. Instead, Jonathan pressed past the opposition to see David for who he truly was—the anointed king.

This is what healthy soul attachments do—they call both participants up higher to be everything God has designed. Rather than trapping or ensnaring us, these relationships cause our souls to soar to new heights. These are the people you want journeying alongside of you on the road to your destiny. Remember, purpose is God's predestined assignment; destiny is your decision. Whether or not you walk in alignment with God's purpose and shape your destiny accordingly depends on who is walking alongside of you and what they are calling you into. Do they see and call out your dysfunction, or do they summon forth your destiny?

ONE STEP TOWARD RESILIENCY

As we journey through life, we all need traveling companions—those who strengthen us when we are weary, who laugh with us when we are happy, who cry with us when we are sad, who give wisdom in the midst of perplexing situations, and whose treatment of us lets us know that we are a soul worth celebrating. Make time to celebrate the soul mates and journeying companions in your life!

You may have few traveler-companions in your life who fit this description. Perhaps there is *no one* in your life whom you would describe as a "soul mate" or journeying companion.

- Evaluate your circle of friends and try to identify these person(s). Be intentional about cultivating those relationships—they may play a role in helping you fulfill your destiny.

- If you do not have a journeying companion, ask God to send you such a person. Perhaps they are already in your life and you have yet to discern who they are.

What is a friend? A single soul dwelling in two bodies. —Augustine

STRATEGIES FOR BREAKING CYCLES AND BUILDING BOUNDARIES

From one man he created all the nations throughout the whole earth. He decided beforehand when they should rise and fall, and he determined their boundaries. —ACTS 17:26 NLT

You can rewrite your life story by breaking old cycles and establishing new boundaries.

SUMMARY

This session is unique as it features two topics. Usually, one topic per session is sufficient, as the goal is not to overload you with too much information. However, with *breaking cycles* and *building boundaries*, it is absolutely essential these concepts are presented as an interrelated pair. When breaking negative cycles in our lives, we must not neglect the importance of building new boundaries.

Boundaries are the context in which your freedom becomes a continuous lifestyle. The enemy looks for people who break cycles of bondage but do not follow up by building clear, definable boundaries. He knows that he can move in quickly, to once again bring you into captivity if the proper boundaries for sustaining freedom have not been established.

Deny the enemy access or entry into your life by establishing clear boundaries once you break any cycle of bondage.

LEARN

Watch Session 6 of the *Reclaim Your Soul* video series.

DISCUSS

Engage your group in conversation using the following questions.

1. Reflect on the story of "the woman at the well" found in John 4. How might have joining herself with a series of lovers created soul ties in her life? Could these soul ties be responsible for the state that Jesus found her in when they met at the well?

2. Define a "cycle" in regard to soul ties. What do you think it means to be trapped in a cycle?

3. How do our relationships help us break cycles or keep us entrapped in cycles?

4. Discuss each of the four strategies for breaking cycles. Ask four different group members to share about a strategy they plan to implement (or have used in the past) to help break cycles in their lives.

5. What does it mean to "adjust your relationships to reflect who you really are"?

6. Why is it important to establish clear boundaries after breaking a negative relationship cycle?

7. What does it say about someone who does not have clearly defined boundaries?

8. What strategies for building boundaries will you start implementing in your life?

EMPOWER (15-20 MINUTES)

Identifying Cycles and Building Boundaries

Today's activity is two-fold.

Consider 1) one cycle-breaking strategy you can begin implementing in your life, and 2) one strategy for building boundaries.

On a piece of paper, create two columns.

CYCLE BREAKING STRATEGY	BOUNDARY BUILDING STRATEGY
Write out the specific strategy that Dr. Trimm shared that is most relevant to your life and situation right now.	*Write down a specific boundary-building strategy you will implement as you break destructive cycles in your life.*

First, we must break the harmful cycles that keep us in the place of bondage. However, it is absolutely important that every cycle that we break is immediately followed up with an established boundary.

At the end of the activity, share what strategy you plan to implement and which corresponding boundary you will build.

SUSTAIN

This week, for about five minutes each day, you will be going through brief exercises. You will be focusing on specific Scripture verses for daily reflection and meditation.

Day Twenty-Six

CAUGHT UP IN THE CYCLE

The woman answered and said, "I have no husband."
Jesus said to her, "You have well said, 'I have no
husband,' for you have had five husbands, and
the one whom you now have is not your husband;
in that you spoke truly."—JOHN 4:17-18

Life happens in cycles. You have the cycle of a day, which repeats every 24 hours. There are monthly, seasonal, and annual cycles. Within these time frames, if you want to change bad cycles, you must take the time to examine what you are doing from day to day, month to month, seasonally, and yearly. This week, we are going to take an in depth look at the John 4 account of the woman at the well. On an ordinary day, at an ordinary well, doing an ordinary task, this woman met Jesus and it changed her "ordinary" into "extraordinary."

Each day this week, we will explore a different aspect of the story that is applicable to our journey of breaking cycles and building new boundaries. Today, we will look at the condition we find her in upon meeting Jesus.

The first thing we notice is that she was a woman clearly caught in a cycle that she could not break free from. Her present was the byproduct of her past. She never rewrote her mental script, and as a result she continued to believe the cycle of deception that kept her snared in a cycle of adultery, fornication, and divorce.

Maybe she moved forward in life, but she never moved on. In other words, she managed to move past a previous husband or lover, but instead of experiencing stability and true love she went from man to man. Again, this is because she could not move on with her life. She was caught in a cycle that was created and fortified by the multiple soul ties she allowed over the years.

A key strategy to breaking cycles in your life is *rewriting your life story by making destiny-enhancing relationship decisions.* Unfortunately, if we continue to focus on how deep we believe we are caught in a cycle or system, it becomes difficult to even consider a life beyond the bars.

ONE STEP TOWARD RESILIENCY

You don't have to stay in the cycle.

Pause and consider any cycles you believe yourself to be trapped in. These are often indicated by repeated behaviors, addictions, or ensnaring relationships.

Let today be the day you decide to move on and rewrite your life story.

> **Soul ties and attachments sustain the cycles of bondage in our lives.**

_____

_____

_____

_____

_____

CYCLES ARE EXPOSED, NOT CONDEMNED

Those who enter into Christ's being-here-for-us
no longer have to live under a continuous, low-
lying black cloud. A new power is in operation.
The Spirit of life in Christ, like a strong wind,
has magnificently cleared the air, freeing you from
a fated lifetime of brutal tyranny at the hands
of sin and death. —ROMANS 8:1-2, MSG

Let's revisit the exchange between Jesus and the Samaritan woman He met at the well.

It is important to notice that Jesus did not condemn her. He did not shame her. He did not rub her sin and past failures in her face. He did not point out her bondage or cycle and use it against her. The fruit of her encounter with Jesus was absolute freedom. We know what happens on the other side. The woman becomes instrumental in testifying about Jesus among her people (see John 4:28-30). Do you think this would have been her response if Jesus had approached her with condemnation? Absolutely not. She would have felt unworthy and perhaps ashamed to share what she learned in encountering Christ.

Condemnation dis-empowers, while godly conviction and confrontation empowers.

So many of us have bought into a lie concerning Jesus' strategy for confronting cycles of addiction and bondage. He confronts, not condemns. Condemnation would do us no good, for condemnation is the powerless counterfeit of conviction. Conviction is the supernatural means through which the Holy Spirit reveals the areas of our lives that need adjusting. We need not fear His conviction, but celebrate it. With His conviction also comes His empowerment to produce transformation. With divine confrontation comes the supernatural empowerment to break every cycle that keeps us bound—for it is *for freedom* that *Christ has set us free*! (See Galatians 5:1 NIV.)

ONE STEP TOWARD RESILIENCY

Have you held back from sharing your struggles with God in fear of condemnation? If so, today is your day for complete honesty and transparency.

Meditate on the following Scriptures before you pray:

> *There is therefore now no condemnation to those who are in Christ Jesus* (Romans 8:1).

> *Let us therefore come boldly to the throne of grace, that we may obtain mercy and find grace to help in time of need* (Hebrews 4:16).

> *And Jesus said to her, "Neither do I condemn you"* (John 8:11).

You can come before God boldly and celebrate the conviction of the Holy Spirit! Celebrate it, because when He reveals a cycle in your life that needs to be broken, *expect* that with the conviction will come the power to make the transformation.

Write down whatever He shares with you during this time of open and transparent prayer. Do *not* be afraid to write down what He shares.

In fact, next to whatever cycle or bondage or stronghold or sin He reveals, *write down* that *"through the Holy Spirit, God has given me the power and ability to break this cycle—not by my own ability, but because of the Spirit of God living inside of me!"*

> **Condemnation dis-empowers. Godly conviction and confrontation empowers us to accomplish what the Holy Spirit is revealing.**

_____

_____

_____

_____

_____

_____

_____

_____

_____

_____

_____

_____

_____

_____

_____

INTRODUCING A CYCLE-FREE REALITY

The Spirit of the Lord is upon me, because he hath anointed me to preach the gospel to the poor; he hath sent me to heal the brokenhearted, to preach deliverance to the captives, and recovering of sight to the blind, to set at liberty them that are bruised, to preach the acceptable year of the Lord. —LUKE 4:18-19, KJV

The Gospel is a message of empowerment and freedom—of how to break free and stay free. When Jesus opened the book and read out of Isaiah 61—introducing His public ministry— He introduced us to a supernatural system that broke chains, released captives, healed disease, restored sight, and announced the year of God's favor! In short, the Gospel is our introduction to living free from soul-binding cycles.

This is what transpired between the Samaritan woman at the well and Jesus. He brought her into a divine collision with a new reality of freedom. The Messiah was standing before her. She was speaking, face to face, with the Chain Breaker. Even as they talked, His very words were breaking age-old religious structures and attachments.

Look at their conversation in John 4. Statement after statement, Jesus' announcements introduce this woman to new paradigms, options, and realities for her life and people:

- (verses 7-9) Jesus spoke to a Samaritan woman. This broke a relational cycle of animosity between Jews and Samaritans, as Jews would not talk with Samaritans. He was introducing her (and ultimately, her people) to a new paradigm of relationship and acceptance.

- (verses 10-15) Jesus defined *true* satisfaction. In the discussion about water, the woman was thinking naturally, while Jesus was introducing her to a spiritual water that would satisfy the deep parts of her soul—the parts that sought satisfaction in soul ties and dysfunctional relationships.

- (verses 19-24) Jesus redefined worship. Perhaps thinking that she could change the subject, the woman gets theological with Jesus and asks Him about physical places to worship. *What's the right one?* Jesus demolishes the old cycles, announcing that standing before her was the solution to the question of *where to worship* (verse 26). It ceased being about *where* and was all about *who* and *how*—by worshiping the Father in spirit and in truth (verse 23).

Jesus Christ, the Cycle-Breaker, lives inside of you through the Holy Spirit. His blood broke the cycle of sin over your life. His Spirit broke the cycle of powerlessness. Now, it is time for you to come into agreement with the Cycle-Breaking Savior. It is His delight and joy. It's what He does.

ONE STEP TOWARD RESILIENCY

Agree with the Word of God, not the message of your cycle.

The Gospel is an authoritative, empowering message that breaks every destructive cycle in your life. The problem is, many of us do not view the Gospel in this manner and thus do not appropriate its cycle-breaking ability.

If the Gospel exposes you to realities of freedom, liberty, peace, joy, functional relationships, courage, healing, etc., make the Gospel the *final word* for your life.

Your cycles convey messages too. They say:

- "You will *never* get out of this."

- "This is how it's *always* going to be."

- "Don't bother trying to get free—you've tried before and failed."

These are lies the enemy uses to keep you bound.

Agree with what God says about you and your cycles—which is ultimately this:

If the Son sets you free, you are free through and through (John 8:36 MSG).

66 *The Gospel sets us free from soul-binding cycles.* 99

_____

_____

_____

_____

_____

_____

Day Twenty-Nine

KEEP THE ENEMY OUT
OF YOUR HOUSE

When an unclean spirit goes out of a man, he goes through dry places, seeking rest, and finds none. Then he says, "I will return to my house from which I came." And when he comes, he finds it empty, swept, and put in order. —MATTHEW 12:43-44

After we encounter the Cycle-Breaker, we must do our part. Shifts must be made. Adjustments. We cannot enjoy a blessing while trying to live the same way we did before. This sets us up for inevitable demonic reentry and infiltration.

People will experience deliverance, healing, and freedom for a season—but don't close the loop. In our fast-food approach to life, we become complacent. We settle for "good enough" and never rise up to fully claim all that God has provided. We may receive a healing when we trust God wants us healed. We may accept deliverance when we choose to live delivered. We experience a *touch* of freedom when we could be *living free*.

The problem is, when we become content with coasting on an experience or one-time breakthrough, we set ourselves up to perpetuate the cycle. Jesus explains this in Matthew 12, making

117

it clear that *we* need to do something about our infrastructure after we receive a touch from God. The enemy is looking for emptiness. He is looking for a life without boundaries that he can exploit and ensnare. His tactics are cyclic. If he can keep the people of God from making forward progress in fulfilling purpose, he has attained victory.

We will experience forward momentum in life to the extent that we build clear and protective boundaries. The video session and *Reclaim Your Soul* book provide more detailed explanation on how to do this, but the point here is to help you recognize the dire need for boundaries. Many of us blame the devil for everything, when in many cases we rolled out a red carpet for his interference in our lives. It's time to slam the door and keep it shut.

Tomorrow, we will cover some strategies on *how* you can build better boundaries. Just remember, people are not your enemy; they are merely tools that satan uses to continue the cycle of bondage in your life. Decide today that enough is enough. You are not going to give him a house to dwell in anymore!

ONE STEP TOWARD RESILIENCY

In what areas of your life do you feel like you have experienced freedom?
Write down some of the key cycles that you believe God has broken or is breaking. It is very important to pay attention to this list, as these are areas God will help you maintain victory if you ask Him—as well as show you how to help others.

At the same time, these are also areas the enemy will try to exploit. Don't give him the opportunity.

Ask the Holy Spirit to give you wisdom and direction on how to build boundaries that protect your freedom, peace, joy, healing, deliverance, etc.

> " *We experience forward momentum in life to the extent that we build clear and protective boundaries.* "

Day Thirty

PATCH UP THE HOLES

Because of laziness the building decays,
and through idleness of hands the house
leaks. —Ecclesiastes 10:18

A decaying building and leaking house are perfect examples of a life without boundaries. When we allow anyone or anything into our lives—including the deepest, most intimate parts—it is like the "house" of our life begins to deteriorate and leak. Laziness produces a life without boundaries, so we must make every effort to overcome this tendency if we are going to walk in sustained freedom.

Boundaries patch up the holes in your life, protecting them from "leaks." The empty places that were previously filled with addiction and bondage are the enemy's primary targets. They become like holes in the structure of your life that, if not tended to, give the enemy access. This statement is not intended to scare you, but to increase your awareness of your adversary's tactics.

This is why you intentionally establish clear, protective boundaries in your life.

Here are a few strategies you can follow, starting in the area of relationships:

- Set clear criteria for the people you allow into your life. Remember, if someone is attracted to you or interested in building a relationship with you, this does *not* obligate you to enter into relationship with them. When we allow just anyone access into our lives, we are being lazy and setting our house up for leaks.

- Create a trust circle; distancing people who would have a negative influence on you. There are people who have earned the position to be closer to you in the circle, while there are others who have likewise demonstrated they should be distanced.

- Develop non-negotiables for your relationships. These are qualities you expect to be exhibited toward you in a relationship context. *Trustworthiness. Confidentiality. Respect. Loyalty. Faithfulness.* All of us make mistakes. However, there are some people who simply do not abide by these types of necessary expectations.

ONE STEP TOWARD RESILIENCY

Identify a boundary that you can start building in your life today! (Choose from one of the three listed above.)

Depending on what the boundary is, *write out* what it means specifically for you and your life.

- What are some *clear criteria* for evaluating prospective relationships and friendships in your life?

- Who is in your *trust circle*? Are there people who should be further away or closer to you in the circle?

- What are your *non-negotiables*? These are the characteristics and qualities that you uphold as essential. If others cannot respect these non-negotiables, don't pursue a relationship with them.

> " *Boundaries patch up the holes in your life, protecting you from 'leaks.'* "

Session Seven

THE POWER OF ENCOUNTERING CHRIST

For I am not ashamed of the gospel of Christ, for it is the power of God to salvation. —ROMANS 1:16

The Gospel is a message of empowerment.

SUMMARY

An encounter with Christ changes everything. In this session, you will continue to study John 4 where the Samaritan woman has a life-changing moment with Jesus at Jacob's well.

Bondage is all about restricted options. Many people remain in a state of bondage because the enemy keeps them blind to the option of freedom. It demands an intersection with the power of God to make us aware that maybe, just maybe, there is life beyond the prison cell that we have known for far too long.

Get ready to discover how the Gospel is a message of empowerment and why it is necessary for you to get back in the driver's seat of your own life. This sounds strange, as the ultimate goal for a believer should be to yield everything to Jesus Christ. Such is absolutely correct. The problem is that many believers have given parts of themselves away to other people and things.

This makes it difficult to stand before God and say, "I give you everything," when in fact we don't have everything *on hand* to give Him. God absolutely uses what we do give Him and He honors this. However, if we want to enjoy the unrestricted power of Heaven flowing in and through our lives, we need to reclaim what we have given away. Only then can we come before the Savior and truly *surrender all.*

LEARN

Watch Session 7 of the *Reclaim Your Soul* video series.

DISCUSS

Engage your group in conversation using the following questions.

1. Consider the story of "the woman at the well" found in John 4. How does this woman's encounter with Christ give her new options?

2. Discuss the six benefits of an encounter with Christ. How have you personally experienced these benefits in your life.

3. How does an encounter with Christ make you aware that *you* have options?

4. What does the following statement mean to you: "A dis-empowered person is a dangerous person"?

5. Why is it vitally important for *you* to be in the driver's seat of your life?

6. How does reclaiming your personal power work together with surrendering control of your life to the Holy Spirit?

EMPOWER (15-20 MINUTES)

Reflect quietly on the following questions for the next 10 to 15 minutes.

Who is in control of your life?

This exercise is absolutely essential in helping you identify where your personal power currently is. Remember, you cannot give something to God—wholly and effectively—if you don't have it first.

Individually, between you and God, reflect on the following questions. Write down your answers in the lined space below.

Who has your personal power?

- Do you have it? If so, it's time to surrender it to Jesus.

- Does someone else? If they do, you need to get it back.

- Or are you successfully and willingly surrendering all to Christ? (The key is to continually live in this place of daily yielding and surrender.)

_____

_____

_____

_____

_____

_____

_____

_____

_____

_____

_____

SUSTAIN

This week, for about five minutes each day, you will be going through brief exercises. You will be focusing on specific Scripture verses for daily reflection and meditation.

MADE AWARE OF WHAT YOU HAVE GIVEN AWAY

The woman said to Him, "Sir, I perceive
that You are a prophet." —JOHN 4:19

Returning to our text in John 4, we watch the Samaritan woman experience a powerful "a-ha" moment during her encounter with Jesus. Her recognition of Jesus' prophetic abilities follows His evaluation of her present state. Without resorting to condemnation, Jesus describes her condition of dysfunction, moving from man to man and presently being with one who is not even her husband.

Her response is interesting. She does not become defensive. She does not get angry. She does not reject what Jesus is saying, thus shutting down the conversation. She perceives that He is a prophet because, as a prophet would do, he calls out her true condition. This does not place her under the yoke of condemnation. We know this because of her response *after* her encounter with Christ.

She does not cower in shame and return to her old life, but becomes a dynamic evangelist for the now-present Messiah. In her encounter with Christ, the woman is made aware of what she has given away, time after time, in relationship after relationship. Her "a-ha" moment is divinely initiated. It does not produce condemnation, but releases empowerment. The Savior of the World—God Incarnate—stood before this woman. Yes, He called out her condition, but only for the purpose of making her understand that *where* she was paled in comparison to *who* she was. Even though she was a Samaritan, Jesus did not respond to her as such. She was a woman at a time when women were not highly regarded in that cultural context, but Jesus nevertheless approached her and engaged her in conversation. This revealed *who* she was—a soul possessing great value and purpose in the sight of God.

This encounter with Christ made her "come to herself." She did not merely leave the encounter touched, but transformed. She did not go back the way she came, going back to a cycle of fornication, adultery, and relational dysfunction. Scripture tells us that, instead, she returned to her village, inviting the people: *"Come see a man who knew all about the things I did, who knows me inside and out"* (John 4:28-29 MSG).

ONE STEP TOWARD RESILIENCY

Get alone with Jesus—and ask Him to make you aware of what you have given away.

Remember, He does not operate using condemnation, guilt, or shame. These are the works of the enemy.

Instead, the Holy Spirit gently reveals areas of your life that you may have given away for the purpose of helping you reclaim who you are and be everything that God has designed you to be.

Write down any areas the Holy Spirit reveals to you.

Then ask Him to give you a glimpse of your *true* identity—how *He* sees you—who you are in His sight.

Just as the woman at the well was a valued, purpose-endowed daughter of God, you too have value. You are significant. You have divine purpose assigned to your life.

This is how you are instructed by God to define yourself. Anyone who disagrees should be avoided at all costs.

> 66 *Encounters with Christ are divine 'a-ha' moments.* 99

_____

_____

_____

_____

_____

_____

_____

_____

_____

_____

_____

_____

_____

_____

_____

_____

Day Thirty-Two

INTRODUCING NEW OPTIONS

*Jesus said to her, "Woman, believe Me, the hour is coming when you will neither on this mountain, nor in Jerusalem, worship the Father." —*John 4:21

An encounter with Christ exposes us to new options. This is key to breaking cycles, cancelling soul ties, and living a resilient life. Resiliency is on the other side of you being aware that there are multiple options. In fact, if anyone tries to shield you from options, making it seem like a relationship with them is *not* optional, you are treading dangerous ground. It is worth repeating that you *always* have options.

We looked at this briefly earlier in our study, but it is worth revisiting here for the subject at hand. Jesus was all about introducing new options to people—particularly those in bondage, in sin, or those enslaved to religious systems. He introduced the option of a Spirit-filled life by being filled with the Holy Spirit Himself and becoming our template. He introduced the option of a Kingdom lifestyle through the *Sermon on the Mount*. He introduced options of not returning evil for evil, not judging, loving your enemy, avoiding adultery at the heart level, etc.

Jesus' entire earthly ministry consisted of exposing humanity to the options His Kingdom provided. This is what took place during his encounter with the Samaritan woman in John 4:21. He started giving her options that were previously unknown to her. Her mind was bound to a concept of worship that Jesus completely demolished. He removed the ceiling from her perspective, thus giving her a new vision of what worship looked like.

In the same way, when you encounter Jesus, you will constantly be exposed to new options. This is the key to avoiding bondage and soul ties, particularly those created through relationships. Dysfunctional people try to convince you that you are without options and that you must stay in a particular role or relationship. In the Kingdom of God, your option is a *life free from bondage.* Anyone who tries to diminish your options is ultimately trying to bind your soul. Prevent this by living a life in God's presence, ever exposed to the options of freedom, liberty, joy, and peace as revealed through His Word.

ONE STEP TOWARD RESILIENCY

Are there people or situations in your life that are trying to blind you to other options?

Any area of your life where you sense bondage or restriction, ask yourself: "Is this person/situation trying to convince me that I am without options?" If so, take this opportunity to get in the Presence of God (see James 4:7).

Grab your Bible or have a computer or tablet handy, and look up verses that will help with your situation.

Simply start by looking up Scripture passages that talk about freedom. This is God's will for you! This is His option. Anything that tries to rob your freedom must be resisted!

As you encounter Jesus, you are constantly exposed to new options.

THE POWER TO RECLAIM AND LIVE RESILIENTLY

I am the Vine, you are the branches. When you're joined with me and I with you, the relation intimate and organic, the harvest is sure to be abundant. Separated, you can't produce a thing. —JOHN 15:5, MSG

Jesus is basically saying, *"Apart from me you can do nothing"* (John 15:5 NIV). Everything we have studied so far is absolutely impossible apart from the energizing power of God working in your life. The Holy Spirit is the One who helps us recognize the cycles that need to be broken. He gives us the wisdom and direction we need to build new boundaries in our lives. He is the Chain-Breaker—the Holy Spirit is the *power source* of the Kingdom of God. Jesus made it possible for us to remain in a continuous state of being joined with Him—intimately and organically. He did this by sending the Holy Spirit, who lives within us. Apart from His indwelling power, in and of our own ability, we could not produce a thing.

It is very important for us to have an understanding of God's power in the process of reclaiming our souls. Think about it.

The Gospel is all about empowerment, from beginning to end. From being born again by the power of God to living every day through the same power and grace, we are totally reliant on His ability to work in and through us to accomplish anything of true significance.

- It was the *power* of God that was demonstrated through the weakness of the cross, for in Jesus' weakest moments, the power of sin, death, and hell were broken.

- It was the *power* of God that raised Jesus from the dead, demonstrating His complete victory and giving us a picture of the life we are called to walk out in Him—one of resurrection power.

- It was the *power* of God that opened Heaven on the Day of Pentecost, releasing the Holy Spirit— God Himself—to live inside of every believer.

You have options—and one of the most significant options is choosing to live an empowered life. As you increase in clarity concerning this truth, don't allow anyone or anything to keep you from the empowerment Jesus died for you to have.

ONE STEP TOWARD RESILIENCY

Who or what is trying to dis-empower you?

Perhaps there are situations you currently are in. Deals you have made. Agreements you have entered. Friendships you have tolerated. Relationships that are life draining. Anything or anyone trying to prevent you from living an empowered life is, ultimately, keeping your soul from flourishing.

These ties must be identified and severed.

Ask the Holy Spirit to reveal these exchanges. Write down any situation or person you sense is trying to dis-empower you, and pray over this list.

- Maybe some people need to be distanced in your trust circle.

- Perhaps some people need to be completely removed.

- You may be too involved in a situation and need to distance yourself.

> **"The Gospel is all about empowerment, from beginning to end."**

_____

_____

_____

_____

_____

_____

_____

_____

_____

_____

_____

_____

_____

_____

_____

Day Thirty-Four

BACK IN THE DRIVER'S SEAT

*I beseech you therefore, brethren, by the mercies
of God, that you present your bodies a living
sacrifice, holy, acceptable to God, which is
your reasonable service.* —ROMANS 12:1

You cannot offer what you do not first possess. Many of us are
familiar with Paul's instruction here, to offer up our lives to
God as a *living sacrifice*. What is a sacrifice? It is an offering with
significant cost. In context, Paul is basically saying that everything that makes us *who we are* should be placed on the altar and
offered up to God, freely and without reservation. This is absolutely true. And there is nothing more beautiful than a life that
burns with the fire of God and carries the fragrance of Heaven.

In focusing on this type of language, we sometimes neglect
the obvious—which I believe is foundational to living in resilience and freedom. Think of it. Christians, week after week,
make commitments to the Lord. They have an "altar experience" where they come forward and recommit their lives afresh
to Jesus. I celebrate and encourage this. However, it is easy to
come to an altar; it is not so easy to actually *give something away* at
the altar. Paul is calling for nothing less than *all* of us presented
before God.

Many of us do not walk in consistent freedom because when we try to "give" our lives to Jesus, we are unable to wholly give ourselves. Why? Because we have not reclaimed our whole selves back from other people, places, and things. We have not broken free from the soul ties and attachments that keep our truest selves imprisoned.

This is a very important topic of discussion. By no means am I saying that Christians who have soul ties or attachments cannot walk in *measures* of sacrifice, surrender, and victory. Unfortunately, if our souls are still bound up with things from our past or mistakes from our present, it becomes very difficult to give all of ourselves away when we do not currently possess all of ourselves. Some of our soul is with *that person*, some of our soul might be locked up in *that contract*, some of our soul got lost in *that experience*, maybe some of our soul is still attached to the occult, etc. These ties do not imply that you are *not* a Christian. They simply restrict you from being a vessel through whom the unlimited power and freedom of Heaven can consistently flow *to* and, ultimately, flow *through*.

Of course, we know that God needs to be in the driver's seat of our lives, but many of us are not even in a place to give Him that control. But be encouraged! This study is all about helping you reclaim your soul so that you have a beautiful, complete offering to give Him.

ONE STEP TOWARD RESILIENCY

Who is in the driver's seat of your life?
Is it you? God? Something or someone else?

- The goal—God.
- The possibility—someone or something else.

Take this time to ask the Holy Spirit to show you *who* or *what* is in control of *your* life.

Write These Down

Ask Him to reveal any people, experiences, or situations you have given parts of yourself to.

Now, through the power of the Holy Spirit, pray and break these attachments.

> *Father, I confess that I have given part of myself to _____. I break this attachment in Jesus' Name and through the power of His blood. I wholeheartedly desire to offer up my entire life as a living sacrifice to You, with nothing held back.*
>
> *I reclaim control over my life for one purpose only—to hand You this control as a willing sacrifice.*
>
> *In Jesus' Name,*
> *Amen.*

> **It might be easy to receive something from an altar, but not so easy to give something away at the altar.**

_____

_____

_____

_____

_____

_____

_____

_____

_____

Day Thirty-Five

FIRST, YOU NEED A CROWN

The twenty-four elders fall down before Him
who sits on the throne and worship Him who
lives forever and ever, and cast their crowns
before the throne. —REVELATION 4:10

Your encounters with Christ introduce you to the only One worthy to steer and direct your life. As you gaze into His eyes of love and unconditional acceptance, you cannot help but *want* to give Him everything. It is not some robotic response. It is not a religious approach either. We love Him because He first loved us. We willingly desire to give Jesus everything knowing He willingly surrendered all for us.

This brings us to a valuable principle found in Revelation 4:10. Too many Christians have the tendency to demonize their humanity and thus, in the process, devalue the soul. Jesus valued the soul. We looked at this at the beginning of our study, where we actually did a comparative analysis, measuring the value of our soul next to the value of everything in the entire world. The world was found lacking next to the preciousness of the human soul.

Your soul is a beautiful crown of offering unto to the Lord. We want it intact. Preserved. Possessed. Not squandered, trampled underfoot, or treated lightly. One day, we will all behold the King of kings and cast our crowns before Him. Everything of value that we ever did, ever received or achieved, we will not be able to hold on to in His presence, for all comes from Him and returns to Him.

Can we treat our soul as such a prized item? As a crown of precious worth in the eyes of God? This is not stretching the text, as this principle surely applies to the soul. Everything that's of value will be cast at His feet. My prayer is that by encountering Christ, you lean in and listen to Him tell you about the value of your soul. He created it. He knit it together. This is your *substance*. Why not take it back so you can have that crown to lay at His feet *now*?

ONE STEP TOWARD RESILIENCY

Is your soul a valuable crown?

Today, simply get into the Presence of Jesus. Ask Him to tell you about the value of your soul.

And then, as you come into greater understanding of how much this precious treasure is worth, freely and willingly lay it at the Savior's feet as an offering of immeasurable worth.

> *Your soul is a beautiful crown of offering unto the Lord.*

Session Eight

RECLAIM YOUR SOUL AND LET THE JOURNEY BEGIN!

*For the Son of man has come to seek and to save that which was lost. —*LUKE 19:10

Like the prodigal son, many of us are looking for what God has already downloaded into our souls. Reclaim Your Soul is all about coming to yourself and recognizing who God created to you to be.

SUMMARY

Reclaiming your soul is the first step to a whole new way of life. The goal of this study has been to take every participant on a journey similar to that of the prodigal son: first, recognizing the value of your soul and its immeasurable worth to God. Second, identifying and confronting the soul ties, attachments, and dysfunctions in your life. Third, breaking cycles that have perpetuated bondage. Fourth, understanding that, after cycles are broken, you need to establish new and clear boundaries.

Information is only a small part of the experience, however. Once we understand truth, we must apply it. Without application, information cannot produce transformation. This is why in the last few sessions we have discussed the essential *next steps*—encountering Christ and now reclaiming your soul.

This session is all about activation. I will lead you in a series of life-changing prayers that will help you take authority over the soul ties and attachments in your life. Everything else you have learned up to this point will help you restructure your mental models and soul habits so you can sustain the freedom gained by having actively reclaimed your soul.

It has been a true privilege being your journeying companion over the past eight weeks. I encourage you not to shelve this study guide and simply let it become another "Bible study you once *did*." My hope is that the notes you took and the reflections you made over these eight weeks are keys to unlocking a lifestyle of sustained freedom and resiliency. This guide is power packed, not necessarily because of anything I've written, but because of what *you* have shared and invested here.

LEARN

Watch Session 8 of the *Reclaim Your Soul* video series.

DISCUSSION

Note: Today, there will be no discussion section. Instead, Dr. Trimm invites you to pray with her.

Even if you feel as though you are not struggling with soul ties, stand in agreement for others seeking breakthrough. Encourage yourself to have ears open to hear the Holy Spirit's voice. He may reveal something during this time that you have not yet realized is limiting you.

EMPOWER (15-20 MINUTES)

Spend the next 10 to 15 minutes in quiet, individual reflection. *What were your "a-ha" moments?*

Recognizing that the subject of soul ties and attachments is intensely personal, it makes sense that you will not want to immediately come out and share about what took place during this time.

Instead, prepare to share the "a-ha" moments that took place over the duration of the eight-week study. What are you taking away from this curriculum experience and what strategies do you plan to implement into your everyday life?

SUSTAIN

This week, for about five minutes each day, you will be going through brief exercises. You will be focusing on specific Scripture verses for daily reflection and meditation.

Day Thirty-Six

COME TO YOURSELF AND TAKE A FIRST STEP

But when he came to himself, he said, "How many of my father's hired servants have bread enough and to spare, and I perish with hunger!" —LUKE 15:17

These five days are not designed to cover the same ground as the video session. The prayer you prayed during the group session is a small part of the experience. While it is necessary, it is what will take place in the days ahead that will prove crucial to implementing what you have discovered over the last eight weeks. Consider these final five reflections my way of helping you begin navigating your new life of resiliency. Thus, we return to the place we started—the prodigal son.

One could say that in Luke 15:17, the prodigal had a major "a-ha" moment. The language is so descriptive of what took place in his soul. We see that he came to "himself." Before he could reclaim his soul and live resiliently, he had to have a very real confrontation with the fact that *the true him* was missing. Did you experience that during the past eight weeks? This is why people often say, "I just don't feel like *myself.*" Their conditions do not demand medical attention, but rather, soul-introspection.

149

This is what took place as the son paused and *honestly* considered his present cycle of bondage—a candid observation of his current condition. His life had become the sum of the soul attachments he had made with the citizen of the country and perhaps a host of other people along the way. He finally assessed the value of his soul, compared it to where he was, and woke up to the reality that things were the way they were because *he was the way he was*. Was this the case with you?

The most powerful "a-ha" moment comes when you understand that you have the ability to change things. No, everything will not shift in an instant. Your decision is not a magic wand. However, it is the vital first step toward fulfilling the purpose God has ordained for your life. Without the first step forward, you remain stuck where you are. Even if you prayed. Even if you verbally broke soul ties. Even if you went through this eight-week study. When you come to yourself, it demands a decision and a step forward. One single step. Not ten. Not even five. And you know what? You have taken a very significant step already. Your decision to confront your condition and break the cycle has been absolutely pivotal in moving toward a lifestyle of resiliency.

Now, it is time to start making *new* decisions that take you in *new directions*.

ONE STEP TOWARD RESILIENCY

What new decision can you make today that will steer your life in a new direction?

After going through the sessions, daily exercises, and finally, the *reclaim* prayer, ask the Holy Spirit this simple question—*what is the first step I need to take?*

Write down whatever the Holy Spirit impresses on your heart. This is your first step.

Remember, a *first* step is all that is required now. Not seven steps. Not ten steps.

One step today. Another step tomorrow.

Soon, you will discover that destiny is simply a series of "one step at a time" decisions moving you toward your created purpose.

You have reclaimed your soul. Now, it's time to begin a glorious new journey where freedom becomes the norm, not the exception.

> *The most powerful 'a-ha' moment comes when you understand that you have the choice to change your life.*

Day Thirty-Seven

ARISE

I will arise and go to my father. —LUKE 15:18

Basically, *coming to yourself* is the process that took place over the last seven weeks. Now, it is time to respond as the prodigal son did—and *arise*. In other words, he intentioned in his mind, with his mouth, and through his actions to leave where he was and return to his father's house. Surprisingly, many people do not recognize the power of this simple yet essential step.

Arise in your mind. Throughout our time together, we have discussed the necessity to rewrite your mental scripts. Usually when someone *comes to themselves* or comes to their senses, this awakening takes place in the soul (your mind is part of the soul). For the believer, the mind recognizes the chasm that existed between the transformation that took place in the spirit—when they were born again—and their present state of life. Our mind is impacted—an impression is made—as it embraces the need to align our lifestyle with our true identity in Christ. This all begins in our thought lives. We must actually think that we are *who* God says we actually are.

Arise in your mouth. Once we start thinking a certain way, we need to ensure that our words agree with our new mental scripts. There is power in declaration. Your words create worlds and shape realities. Your tomorrow is often the result of the words spoken *today*. When we speak forth what our minds are now meditating on, concerning our true identity, we are reinforcing what we believe. It's not just saying positive words or simply thinking "happy things." It is becoming so convinced that you are who God designed you to be that your mouth cannot counter it.

Arise in your actions. Once our minds start believing we are who God says we are and our mouths speak it out, we must back up both with a corresponding lifestyle. This is why Jesus was so intentional about describing the power of being a *doer* and not a hearer only. The journey we have taken over the last seven weeks was partly targeted at your mind. You need to adjust the way you think in order to adjust the way you live. However, we cannot be satisfied with an enriched mind without a transformed life. Such is not biblical. The renewed mind and empowered mouth are aimed at producing a transformed lifestyle.

To arise is not to become someone new—someone who is not you. No. To arise is to mentally, verbally, and demonstratively step into the identity God assigned to you before the foundation of the world. It is truly a high or *upward* calling that demands you to arise in order to fully step into it (see Phil. 3:14).

ONE STEP TOWARD RESILIENCY

Think different, speak different, and live different. This is what it means to truly *arise*.

Could things be the way they are because you…

- *think* the thoughts you do?
- *speak* the words you speak?

Now that you have discovered *who you are*…

- how will you think differently?
- how will you speak differently?

Think differently.
Speak differently.
Live differently.

Day Thirty-Eight

REPENT

*I will arise and go to my father, and will
say to him, "Father, I have sinned against
heaven and before you."* —LUKE 15:18

Repentance is two-fold. It is experiencing a healthy, godly sorrow over sin, but it is also a transformative invitation into a complete "about-face" in life. Repentance is completely empowered by the Holy Spirit, but it is an act of your redeemed will. Think of it this way. Without the Holy Spirit living inside of you, your *free will* remains enslaved to sin. You are not able to just "will up" the power to repent. But because God lives inside of you and because the Spirit empowers you to do what cannot be done *naturally*, at any time, you are able to assess your present situation, confess your sin, break your ties, and do a complete "about-face" in life.

This "about-face" is "soulular" in nature. In fact, it is amazing how much of the soul repentance impacts. For transformation on the outside to take place, who we are on the inside must be changed. As a believer, your spirit man is sealed by the Holy Spirit. However, your soul is *being* washed by the water of God's word. It is a lifelong journey. Your mind—a dimension of your soul—is being renewed and transformed daily. We looked at this yesterday. Remember, the result of thinking differently and speaking differently is *living* differently.

The problem with repentance is that many people so strongly emphasize the "godly sorrow over sin" that the next steps are never taken. Mourning is healthy for a season. But a time comes when we need to take the next step. In the same respect, mourning over our sin is healthy, but only to the degree it motivates us to do the "about-face" in life and embrace everything Jesus died to give us.

Repentance is the process of bringing your soul into agreement and alignment with the transformation that occurred in your spirit. Even though Christ is present in your spirit, He is being formed in you daily. This formation process has everything to do with how we respond to the invitation of repentance.

One Step toward Resiliency

Repent—completely.

You have already dealt with your sins, broken soul ties, and confronted dysfunction. Today, we are not going to even deal with those items.

Most certainly, you have already expressed sorrow over these choices and desire to change.

Now, I want to invite you into the next level of repentance— the *about-face.*

Make today a vital, historic day of decision for you.

> *Father, I declare that today is my about-face moment. You have touched my mind. You are changing the way I think and speak about myself. I have confessed my sins to You. You have broken the cycles and soul ties in my life. Now, I step into the life that You have ordained me to live—a resilient life. A free life. A life without bondage.*

I turn my back on the old and step toward the new. I break my connection with the past and move on to embrace all that You have for me.
In Jesus' Name!

> **Repentance positions you to make an "about-face" in life.**

_____

_____

_____

_____

_____

_____

_____

_____

_____

_____

_____

_____

_____

_____

_____

_____

_____

Day Thirty-Nine

RESTORED TO YOUR ORIGINAL IDENTITY

*Then God said, "Let Us make man in Our image, according to Our likeness; let them have dominion." —*GENESIS 1:26

Every step toward reclaiming your true self is celebrated by your Father in Heaven. Why? Because He created you to be *you*. In His original design for creating humanity, soul ties and attachments were never part of the blueprint. They are a result of the Fall and a product of sin. When Adam and Eve gave authority to the devil in the Garden of Eden, they likewise entered into a poisonous soul attachment with sin that would continue from generation to generation.

When Jesus announced that He came to seek and save that which was lost, the language clearly brings to mind the *exchange* that took place in Eden. Something was lost in the transaction between humanity and satan. *Identity.* Mankind was created to govern and rule the earth realm as God's ambassadorial agents (see Gen. 1:26-28). Scripture clearly expresses that *"the heaven, even the heavens, are the Lord's; but the earth He has given to the children of men"* (Ps. 115:16).

Our original identity was completely free of bondage and dysfunctional attachments. In Eden, man lived in perfect union with one another and, most importantly, unbroken fellowship with God. God's original intent reveals His unchanging design. In other words, the function of mankind was never revoked because of sin. Part of what Jesus came to restore was our sense of identity.

We are living in agreement with the most authentic version of ourselves when we are free, liberated, and fully possess our personal power.

ONE STEP TOWARD RESILIENCY

Do you know who you really are?

Have you ever thought about your original created purpose? *Why did God create mankind?*

Review Genesis 1–3. You will see a clear blueprint of who God made humans to be *through* what He assigned them to do. You were created for the purpose of dominion—of ruling and reigning in life, bearing God's image and likeness.

Bondage was never part of this design. Remember this as you step into your new life of freedom. I repeat—*freedom and resiliency should be your norm, not your exception!*

Protect this at all costs as you move forward in your journey to a resilient life.

> *God's original intent reveals His unchanging design.*

Day Forty

REDEEMED AND RECLAIMED

And he arose and came to his father. But when
he was still a great way off, his father saw him
and had compassion, and ran and fell on
his neck and kissed him. —LUKE 15:20

Today is our last day together. I cannot tell you what a joy and honor it has been taking this journey with you. I can't wait to hear your story of how God brought you into a lifestyle of greater resiliency and freedom. Get ready to breathe in new air. *Free air.* No longer will the dark cloud of bondage be following you around like a looming thunderstorm, just waiting to release a torrential downpour on your life. It's gone. You now recognize what soul ties are and will forbid any such attachments from forming again in your life.

While I am proud of the progress you have made, there is One who is cheering you on in a far greater and more valuable measure than I ever could. The Father in Heaven has been waiting for this moment. In fact, He has been both watching and participating in the process. The Holy Spirit has empowered you to go through the process of reclaiming your soul, but the Father has been right there—all along—preparing a celebration to commemorate the true *you* coming back. Just as it happened with the prodigal son, your heavenly Father is rejoicing!

The boy who left that day was not the same boy who returned. When he left, he was self-seeking, arrogant, and above all ignorant, but when he returned to his father's house he was free from all those confines. His father longed for this precious day. As his son walked away, I'm sure he thought, "My son is not acting like himself." But when he saw him returning home, what did he exclaim? *"For this my son was dead and is alive again; he was lost and is found"* (Luke 15:24). The boy standing before him had "come to himself" and was now able to approach him as his son. When at last he had become himself, he was alive again.

If anyone valued you coming to *yourself*, it would be the One who created you. After all, He is the very author of your soul. Demolish any thought that your humanness is evil. God responded to sin so severely through the death of His Son, *not* because He was angry at our humanness, but because He wanted to destroy the very thing that corrupted our humanness. Redemption was purposed to actually restore *true* humanity, which is *you* functioning in the most authentic version of yourself—a man or woman living in the image and likeness of God. This is what you were made for, and *this* is what you have reclaimed!

ONE STEP TOWARD RESILIENCY

Your last step is simply this—keep this guide close to you.

Don't put it away on a shelf somewhere, because this process is *not* finished. It is actually a lifelong journey, and what you have recorded in these pages will be invaluable as you continue to reclaim your freedom.

These are your golden nuggets gleaned from your personal experience throughout this journey—and will continue to guide you forward, onward, and upward.

- You may find it helpful to revisit this process.

- You may need to reference a page, a note, or a power thought.

- You may need to evaluate warning signs of a potential soul tie or attachment.

- You may need to help someone begin their journey to reclaiming their soul.

- You may want to lead a *Reclaim Your Soul* study yourself.

Either way, your notes, your reflections, and your meditations—as recorded in these pages—are *your gift* to yourself. Cherish them and celebrate the progress you have made.

I believe in you and am absolutely thrilled to know that this world will benefit from yet another soul flourishing in freedom and resiliency.

> **If anyone valued you coming to yourself,**
> **it would be the One who created you.**

Additional Notes

Additional Notes

Additional Notes